How to choose a
MONOLOGUE
for any audition

by Karen Kohlhaas

Printed in the U.S.A.
Publisher:
Big & Slow, Inc.
P.O. Box 1587
Old Chelsea Station
New York, NY 10113
Phone: (212) 252-4200
Website: www.monologueaudition.com

Cover design and interior book design
by Jonathan Gullery

FIRST EDITION

ISBN 978-0-9786384-3-6

This book is dedicated to my high school drama teacher

Frederick Leslie Baird

Les Baird kept a well-stocked filing cabinet of plays in the drama room at Cheyenne Mountain High School in Colorado Springs, Colorado. That cabinet, and Baird's excellent teaching and enthusiasm for new plays, are the reasons I knew I should study with David Mamet when I enrolled in New York University's undergraduate drama department. The group of us who studied with Mamet and with William H. Macy became the Atlantic Theater Company, and we are now approaching our 25th year as a company and school.

Also by Karen Kohlhaas

The Monologue Audition: A Practical Guide for Actors
(Foreword by David Mamet)

The Monologue Audition Teacher's Manual

The Monologue Audition Video (DVD)

"The deepest human desire is
the desire for a narrative."

– Francesco Clemente

Contents

CHOOSING MONOLOGUES

MONOLOGUES FOR GROWTH

REPERTOIRE

Afterword

RESOURCES

About the Author

Active vs. Passive Auditioning

I think I was drawn to working with actors on monologues because I saw a lot of agony that I knew could be turned completely around. Much of the agony was focused on rehearsing and auditioning with monologues, but an equal amount seemed to be experienced during the actors' search for material.

Here are the monologue-choosing issues I see actors struggling with the most often:

- Feeling overwhelmed by the amount of writing that is out there—they don't know where to start;

- Feeling intimidated or guilty about not knowing enough plays and playwrights;

- Not knowing what kind of material is best for a particular audition;

- Not having a clear sense of themselves as actors. Including, but also going beyond "type" issues, actors are often unsure about how to factor their personalities into the choices they make for auditions;

- Being so daunted by performing monologues in general that they either avoid monologue auditions completely, or only have one or two pieces—which they often hate—that they use for every audition they go on;

- Because of any or all of the above, procrastination! Actors routinely put off their material searches as long as possible, and end up taking the first monologue that seems acceptable, which is often a very overdone piece from a monologue book.[1]

Have you ever experienced any of these problems? This book focuses on solving all of them.

I teach actors in my New York monologue classes to use the same creative storytelling skills in auditions that they use when performing in a play or in front of a camera. I encourage them to think of monologue auditions—and all other kinds of auditions—as regular parts of their artistic lives, not separate from the rest of their acting.

We also never forget that the business side of the class is about how to audition effectively. We look at all of the verbal and nonverbal communications an actor can make during an audition, and how to make positive and professional choices about each one.

In this book, I'm going to focus on both the artistic and business sides of monologue choice.

I think much of the difficulty actors have when choosing monologues comes from not having a clear and effective way to work on them. It happens often in my classes that once actors

---

1   I am not against monologue books. See "How to Use a Monologue Book."

see what they can actually creatively *do* with an audition piece, using specific acting and directing choices, they see potential in monologues they would have overlooked before.

For information on how I teach monologue preparation, please check out my monologue technique book, DVD, and New York classes[2]. For now, we are going to focus on:

The Art of Choosing Monologues

Choosing monologues *can* be an art—a creative act you can get good at. I have seen many actors learn to do this. The key is to become *active* in your material choice—and your whole approach to auditioning—instead of passive.

The passive actor:

- Has only one or two monologues prepared, and doesn't love them;

- Does those same pieces for all monologue auditions she goes on—or only goes to the auditions for which those pieces could possibly work;

- Hopes that if she acts her pieces well, the auditors will choose her;

- Thinks of her material choice as secondary to her acting ability.

The active actor:

- Understands how his choices of material can make major statements about who he is as an artist, *and* about how much he is in tune with the needs of his auditors;

---

2   For information on the book, DVD and classes, go to www.monologueaudition.com.

- When necessary, is willing to take a few risks to achieve both of these things, which for him is more desirable than staying with the pack;

- Chooses well-written monologues he likes and loves;

- Notes all of the requirements for an audition—style, period, type, length;

- Finds out anything he can about the tastes, preferences, styles, and production history of those who will be watching, and then considers all of those factors plus his own type, strengths, and sensibilities;

- Studies the local industry and trends—even if this is the theater community in a town or small city—to inform his choices;

- Has a repertoire of many monologues, and is enough in practice that working up a new piece, when needed, is not a big deal for him;

- Walks in the door with the best one or two monologues he has been able to find and rehearse for that particular audition;

- Has other pieces he can go to if they want to see more, or see something else.

All of this careful preparation means this actor will be meeting his auditors *actively* in the audition room. Can you see that this is a completely different way to audition than the passive way described above?

It is completely within your power to be this active actor.

You'll have to be ready to put your procrastination about finding monologues aside. However, when you know how to focus your choices of material, your searches for monologues will be much more productive, and this will increase your motivation.

Won't it be a huge relief to replace that feeling of dread with some practical—and often very enjoyable—thinking and reading?

The Two Reasons to Choose Monologues

- **To prepare for specific kinds of auditions (and competitions).** In this case, the priorities are finding material that is a great match for the type of audition, and that showcases you and your current strengths.

- **For artistic development and growth.** Here, your primary purposes are exploration, working on difficulties, building skills, challenging yourself to work out of your comfort zone, and (yes) having fun.

I encourage working on monologues for both these reasons, and find that frequently they can overlap. The pieces you work on for specific auditions *should* engage you as a storyteller, and help you to grow as an artist. It is important though to be conscious of your purpose when working on each monologue, because not every monologue you work on for artistic reasons will serve you in the audition room.

Part of the purpose of this book is to make that distinction very conscious and clear. There are several factors to take into account when choosing audition material, and we will look at each one of them.

Learning to choose well for your auditions is a skill you can practice and improve at. The considerations you'll have to make will require you to step outside yourself and understand more about the audition process.

In this book, I'll present an overview of the factors that should go into choosing monologues. We'll look at monologue choice from the auditors' perspective, and you'll be shown ways of evaluating who you are as an actor and how to factor your type and personality into your choices. I'll examine the many questions that arise about contrasting pieces, cutting and editing, inappropriate material, accents, overdone monologues, and more. I'll discuss material choice for the different kinds of monologue auditions that exist, and also present ways to use monologues for growth and repertoire building. All of this will support you in being an *active* auditioning actor.

How to Choose a Monologue

If there is a basic equation that will help you choose monologues for auditions, I think it's this:

The auditors' purpose in holding the audition[3]

\+ Who you are as an actor and what you have to offer

\+ The auditors' stated requirements

\+ Anything else you can find out about
the auditors' background, tastes, and preferences

= The factors your material choices should actively and
directly address in each audition

Here is the process I suggest for choosing a monologue for
a particular audition. Each item will be discussed in detail in the
following chapters.

---

3   To cast a role or company, to meet new actors, to choose students, or to
find new clients.

First:

- Think about what the audition is for.

- Research *all* aspects of the audition—the place, the project, the people involved.

- Note *exactly* what they've asked for.

Then, look for a piece that:

- Observes all of their stated requirements;

- Is a good monologue;

- Is a good monologue for *you;*

- To the best of the knowledge you have, is in tune with who *they* are, and what they need;

- Using your best judgment, does not have any qualities likely to work against you;

- Using your best judgment, is not something they are likely to see over and over again at these auditions (unless, of course, they *ask* actors to perform frequently-done monologues, or to choose from a list they've published).

Your ultimate goal for an audition is to have material that:

- Features some of your skills positively

and

- Shows how you might best fit into their

    » Show or project

    » Company

    » Conservatory class/ensemble

    » Repertory season

    » Pool of actors they call in

    » Client roster

As you can see, there is room for variations in opinion and taste, which is as it should be. Although I will present some strong opinions, it's important to emphasize that nothing is absolute! There will be auditions at which they don't like the same monologues you do, and auditions at which they may like the monologue but not your interpretation. Or, they may think you did a good job, but just don't see you as that character. Read a set of reviews for almost any play or movie, and you will see one reviewer praising the very elements—acting, direction, writing, and design—that another critic disliked.

It's impossible to get it perfectly right every time—and you are likely to hurt your auditions if you try to. I love this quote:

> *Energy is more important than perfection. Perfection is boring. What's exciting is something that is alive, and things that are alive have flaws.*
>
> —Steven Soderbergh

Instead of trying to please every auditor, get better and better at taking *your* best, most informed, most prepared shot at each audition.

Top Monologue-Choosing Mistakes

Below is an overview of the problems I see actors having with material choice the most often.

The good news: all of these problems are completely solvable. Understanding and avoiding them will help you become a monologue-choosing master.

- **Procrastination.** Waiting until the last minute is the number-one enemy of monologue choice. You know this: the longer you wait, the more painful and stressful the process. Better that you take a few months to build up a kick-ass repertoire, than habitually grab a so-so piece at the last minute.

- **Trying to make one or two monologues do everything for you.** If you hate your monologues, this might be the reason. You're trying to make the same couple of pieces—or even just *one* piece—serve you in too many different kinds of auditions. You are *overworking* them. They are tired. And that is not fun to watch.

- **Firmly believing there is one monologue that can do everything for you, if you could only find it.** This monologue does not exist.

- **Not having a large enough repertoire.** This problem goes hand in hand with the last two. Answer this question honestly: "Do I have monologue choices I'm happy with for most auditions I currently am or could be going on?"

- **Doing overdone material.** There will be discussion later on about when and when not to work on frequently-done or overdone monologues. I polled ten industry professionals about the monologues they see the most.[4] Most overdone monologues come from monologue books, which means actors are not reading enough.

- **Doing age-inappropriate material.** The ten industry professionals also answered questions about other monologue audition issues. Doing age-inappropriate material was the one factor they *all* agreed can work against actors.

- **Doing material you're not quite on top of.** Your audition pieces should feature your strengths, not new skills you are working on. It's also important to know what kind of material falls within your castable range. Later chapters will talk about ways to know when a piece is ready and right to bring into auditions.

- **Not considering what—and who—the audition is *for*.** This is an often-neglected step of the audition process, and can lead to actors bringing

---

4   Results are at www.monologueaudition.com.

in ineffective material. There is much you can learn about your best choice of monologue by doing some research on the purpose of the audition, and the people you'll be in front of.

- **Not bringing in what they asked for.** Choosing monologues that meet auditors' requests is the first way you show them that you listen, that you care about their needs, and that you are a pro.

- **Doing inappropriate monologues.** Sometimes monologues are chosen for their disturbing subject matter or graphic images. These pieces can prevent the purpose of an audition from happening, because they often distract attention from the *acting*.

- **Doing poor writing.** What kind of gas are you putting in your tank? The cheap stuff? Are you doing "junk food" monologues—pieces that are generic, vague, or just plain bad writing?

- **Doing material you dislike.** If you have done this you know what it feels like—a bad date.

- **Asking someone to choose your material for you.** Doing so cuts off your power. Developing your knowledge of, feeling for, and taste in various kinds of writing will exponentially expand your growth as an artist and an actor.

- **Not knowing many plays.** This is a very easy problem to solve.

- **Not reading regularly.** Ditto.

The Best Way
to Find Material

It's obvious: read!

Creating the habit of reading regularly is one of the two most powerful and cost-effective investments you can make in the quality of your experience as an auditioning and working actor.[5]

When we interviewed director Amanda Charlton of the Williamstown Theatre Festival for *The Monologue Audition Video (DVD)*, she talked about how actors who read a lot instantly stand out from those who bring in the same old stuff. She said:

> *"A true artist wants to find the best material—is interested, just plain old interested. And that I can tell right away. [When an] actor comes in with a new piece from a great hot playwright that not a lot of people know, I'm extra-aware of that person—I'm interested in what they're about."*

I could not agree with this statement more. I cannot implore you enough to read plays—for the sake of your own enjoyment, the experience of those who watch your auditions, and for the long-term quality of work that you hope to bring to

---

5   The other is working regularly on your voice.

your audiences. Over a period of time, regularly reading plays will make into you a completely different actor than you would have been if you didn't.

Everyone has to start somewhere, and it does take time to become the empowered actor Amanda described. Here are some suggestions to get you started:

Revisit the Past: Start with Your Inspiration

It's easy to feel overwhelmed when it comes to building a steady reading schedule—where should you begin? I suggest you start by re-reading some of the writing that has most inspired you. Think back to the plays you read—or movies you saw—that were instrumental in making you want to become an actor, and revisit them.

When you do, notice how you feel about these works now. Has your perception changed? Do they still inspire you? Are there works by your favorite writers that you haven't read yet? Which writers influenced *them*, and which writers were influenced *by* your favorites? When you start with your own inspiration and follow these chains of influence, you can set yourself on a path to expand your knowledge of and interaction with the playwrights whose work most speaks to you.

Look into the Future: Think About the Kind of Work You Want to Do

Spend some time writing, thinking, and talking to other artists about the kind of work you want to do during your life as an actor. Are you most happy doing classical plays? Do you love being part of developing new work in rehearsal?

Actors have to worry about so many things: maintaining and improving skills, surviving between acting jobs, fitness and appearance, keeping up with the industry, and much more. Sometimes these concerns can obscure the original threads of inspiration that made you want to be an actor. Sometimes the intense desire just to be cast in *something* can distract you from pursuing the kind of work that most fulfills you.

You can, on a regular and manageable basis, keep notes, lists, and journals of your dream projects and roles. Track your favorite writers, directors, and companies, and keep a list of your "must do" roles. Does thinking of doing this scare you? Dare to do it. Use your results to plan what you should read next. (For more on these kinds of practices, see "Who Are You as an Actor?")

Become a Well-Read Actor

I truly believe all actors need to read plays, even those actors who say they want to concentrate on film and television work.

In the writer and producer credits of the three *Law & Order* television shows (as in countless movie and TV credits), you will see the names of many established *playwrights,* including Warren Leight, Theresa Rebeck, Diana Son, Jerome Hairston, Gina Gionfriddo and Eric Overmeyer.

All forms of creative writing—and our everyday language—have been influenced by the work of great playwrights. More terms from Shakespeare, for example, are featured in our daily expressions than many people realize—everything from "elbow room" *(King John)* to "a fool's paradise" (*Romeo and Juliet*).

Knowing the classics, and being able to recognize how they have influenced modern dramatic writing—including film and television—will give you a deeper understanding of exactly what you are *saying* when you act scenes and monologues. You will understand specific references, you will be more sensitive to dramatic structure, and your taste will become more sophisticated—you'll be able to clearly tell the difference between great, good, mediocre, and just plain terrible writing.

If you haven't opened a Restoration comedy or a Greek tragedy since high school or college (or ever) you might start by looking at an anthology that features plays written in different eras—from ancient times all the way through the 20th century. As you read through the plays, note the ones that most appeal to you. Learn about the history, the culture, and who else was writing. Read more of the works of the playwrights you like best, and pull monologues from these plays whenever you find one that suits you.

The actor Brian Dennehy spoke to our students at the Atlantic Acting School, and said:

> *"Learn about life! Read! Who was Chekhov? Where did he live? What did he do? Shakespeare—what kind of a life did he have? His characters—where did they come from? Arthur Miller? Eugene O'Neill? There's nothing you can ask me about Eugene O'Neill that I don't know."*

Mr. Dennehy talked about his long collaboration with the director (and artistic director of Chicago's Goodman Theatre) Robert Falls. Years ago, they set on a course to work together on some of the great, "hard plays that nobody does." That mission has led to their acclaimed and often award-winning productions of Brecht's *Galileo*, Miller's *Death of a Salesman*, and O'Neill's *A Touch of the Poet*, *The Iceman Cometh*, *Long Day's Journey into Night*, and *Desire Under the Elms*.

Reading Can Inspire You to Greatness
I don't think someone like Brian Dennehy becomes a great actor and *then* decides to find out about magnificent plays and their playwrights. Rather, I believe that reading and knowing a huge breadth of dramatic literature will help you to find and define yourself *within* it as you live and grow as an actor.

Frances McDormand also spoke to our students, and made the beautiful observation that an actress can play the parts in Chekhov throughout her career, starting and finishing with *Three Sisters:* from the youngest sister Irina to the elderly servant Anfisa.

I notice that when I feel dull and uninspired as a director, it's because I haven't read or seen anything great in a while. Reading and seeing excellent stories encourages me to find the plays I want to bring my best to.

When you choose monologues out of a sense of wanting to interact artistically with particular writers, plays, and roles that speak to you, you're a very different actor than the one who drags in a monologue to "fulfill a requirement."

Instead, you are a practicing artist, whom auditors are getting a glimpse of in the course of your artistic life. The other actor is waiting for someone to cast him so his artistic life can begin.

Building the Reading Habit

Always have a play with you.

Reading is a habit that will never be unnecessary in your career. How else are you going to choose the best roles to take? An actor's medium is the written word.

Contrast the not-quite-ready actor with the actor who has made a regular habit of reading plays, both known and less-known, classical to contemporary. She has her finger on the pulse of the most current playwriting. This actor knows the playwrights who are writing roles most suited to her. She keeps lists of her favorite plays and writers. If she is interested in film and television she keeps current with these media too. She also looks off the beaten path for monologues—in novels, editorials, letters, documentaries, and comedy essays. She has a notebook crammed with possibilities that she works on one at a time.

The keys to creating a reading habit, according to Marla Cilley (a.k.a. The Flylady[6]), are:

- **Take baby steps**. Trying to do it all at once will overwhelm you and lead to procrastination.

- **Make reading a routine.** Find regular opportunities in your daily life. Maybe it's while you're commuting, doing laundry, or during one or

---

6   Please see my article "Why Flylady is Great For Actors" at www.mono-logueaudition.com for an introduction to Flylady's extraordinary (and free) system for managing your daily and creative life.

more mornings, afternoons, or evenings you set aside each week.

- **No whining allowed. You can do this.** The 20 seconds you spend complaining about not being able to find a monologue are 20 seconds that are lost forever. Recycle your complaining time into "read it now" time.

Make reading more fun by involving others. Have periodic readings with friends. Hold a "festival" during which you and others watch the plays of a famous writer that were made into movies, and documentaries about that playwright. Have a circle of friends you pass around scripts with.

Setting achievable goals, such as "I want to read all of the plays of Moliere this spring," or, "I want to find three playwrights who write great parts and monologues for me," will also help you build routines and inspire you to keep reading.

It will also greatly help your motivation to have one or more partners with whom you fulfill a regular commitment to rehearse new monologues. I have heard from many pairs and groups of my former students who continue to meet to practice monologues, cold reading, and audition skills. They say that meeting regularly helps them keep their skills sharp, and pays off in their audition results.

Choose Your Own Material

This is my challenge to you as an artist: don't ask anyone to choose your material for you. I do believe in getting opinions from others as part of your rehearsal process, but keep yourself in the driver's seat. It will change the whole way you audition.

An actor who wants someone else to choose his material is an actor who is probably not quite ready to audition seriously. He is not yet in touch with writing that excites him artistically. He is not inclined to do the work it takes to find the best piece for a particular audition—he wants someone else to take this responsibility for him.

It is fine for a new actor to feel like he needs some guidance, but actors who think they're ready to get out there and audition seriously need to already be reading and working on material as part of their everyday creative and professional lives.

No One Has Time for Maybe

An eye-opening perspective on material choice came from a casting experience I had with my friend Paul Marcarelli. Paul is the Verizon ("Can you hear me now?") spokesman of the last several years.

Years ago, I placed an audition notice in *Backstage* magazine for an Off-Off Broadway play I was directing. It was an absurdist play about a bourgeois family. I was casting all roles—a mother, a father, an adult neighbor, a young man, a maid, and a teenage daughter.

I received stacks and stacks of photos. It was overwhelming. I called Paul and said, "I'm sitting here in my living room with the hopes and dreams of 600 actors—I'm paralyzed! How can I decide who to call in just from these pictures and résumés?

Paul came over and was wonderfully practical. He said, "We have to decide on a gut level who to call in, because there are so many pictures. Based on the style of the play, our reactions to the photos, and the experience on the résumés, we are going to sort them into "Yes, No, or Maybe." And that's what we did.

When we finished, we had two relatively small Yes and No piles for each role—about 10% for Yes, and about 20% for No. We had one huge pile for each role—about 70%—for Maybe. I called the Yeses first. Some of the Yeses' acting abilities did not match the promise of their résumés; some looked completely different than their pictures; and some of them were just not

29

right at all, as it turned out. But sorting them that way was a starting point, and it helped me to get on with casting the play.

I did not get to any of the Maybes—I was able to fill the roles from the Yeses who auditioned.

Paul had a revelation while we were sorting those pictures. As the Maybe piles grew many times higher than the Yes and No piles, he said, "Oh my gosh, *I get it*. I want a headshot that puts me on the Yes pile or on the No pile. A headshot that is really, really *me*—not just me trying to look as attractive or acceptable as possible. I want my photo—and my audition—to be specific enough that I am a Yes or a No for a project. Some of these Maybes might be great for the part, but we'll never know, because no one has *time* for Maybe."

I have come to feel exactly the same way about material choice for auditions. As a director I will tell you, and I know other directors will agree, that I would always rather see a *choice*, than an "acceptable effort." Your choice may work or not—it will be a Yes or No for a certain audition. The "acceptable efforts" are often fine, but will stay in the Maybe pile.

This is a principle you see in business and in art—and in life—all the time. Many of us would rather avoid failure and rejection—by staying safely in Maybe—than take a real shot at success.

It is said that the most successful entrepreneurs fail all the time—but they take many more shots and calculated risks[7] than the average businessperson. Enough of their shots succeed to make them some money. And what is an actor but an entrepreneur? Isn't an entrepreneur someone who is willing to put

---

7   Please notice that I said *calculated* risk. When it comes to audition material choice, I don't mean that anyone should make a random, unconnected choice for the sake of trying to be memorable. These choices are seen at auditions all the time, and they work against actors. Real examples from Atlantic EPAs: in one audition, an actor performed a monologue in the "Elvish" language from *The Lord of the Rings* (in an audition for an English-speaking part); in another, an actor had actual fire shoot out of his hands at the end of a monologue on magic. These kinds of choices just look crazy, and can do lasting damage to an actor's chances with his auditors.

in long hours for little or no pay, and no guarantee of success, because she believes so strongly in her product?

Your calculated risk for an audition should involve taking complete stock of the factors involved, and choosing the monologue you think gives you the *best* shot at showing them how you could work together.

In the end, out of the Yeses, they will cast the same amount of actors in the role: one.

If you are not that actor, you often won't know if you got on the Yes, No, or Maybe pile during the casting process. Dealing with that lack of feedback on your efforts can be one of the most frustrating things about being an auditioning actor.

It can be so easy to get stuck in this frustration. But, how you frame the audition process is completely up to you. You can:

- **Learn to satisfy *yourself* with the amount of consideration you put into aiming for the Yes pile.** Crossing into that territory—focusing on your own satisfaction instead of lamenting how unfair, anonymous, and uncommunicative the process is—can totally change and improve the way you audition.

- **Take as many shots at what you want as possible.** Given where you are in your career and what your goals are, follow in the steps of great entrepreneurs: put yourself out there, learn from your successes and failures, and *keep going*.

Returning to these two points of focus when you are frustrated will help re-route your time and energy to actions and efforts that will move you forward.

Paul made an active decision to study the audition process so that he could get good at aiming for the Yes pile. Instead of looking for feedback outside himself, he focused on taking his best shot at each part, based on his research about the type of audition it was and what he thought they would be looking for. He worked on improving his audition skills, material choice, preparation of pieces, and on interacting smoothly with the auditors in the room. He says he even got to enjoy the pressure of getting *close* to being cast: when called back multiple times for a role, he studied how to keep his choices consistent while also improving on each callback.

If you decide, as Paul did, to make this transformation, you might find that you *do* end up getting positive feedback, and getting cast more often.

Raising Your Percentages

People love to quote statistics about how hard it is to succeed as an actor: "Less than 5% of Actors' Equity Association members are working at any given time." "Five years after acting school, less than 10% of the graduates are still in the profession."

Those statistics may be true, but this statistic balances them out: auditors, including me, will tell you that in auditions, 10% or less of actors look like they truly want to be there. And that 10% tends to be made up of the actors who are giving the best auditions.

All of the work I teach is about "raising your percentages" in the audition room. Raising your percentages means that you have to stop "meeting the requirement" and start working to show them who you are at your best. You raise your percentages with:

- **Voice work.** If there are ten actors who can play the role, but one has worked on her voice until it is beautiful, who is going to get the part?

- **Speech work.** If there are ten actors with great voices who can play the role, but one has complete control over his speech—he can sound any way he wants or needs to sound—who is going to get the part?

- **Physical control and expression.** If there are ten actors who can play the role, but one is aligned, grounded and graceful—while the others have various physical habits like fidgeting with their hands, shifting their weight back and forth, or jutting their heads forward when they act—who is going to get the part?

- **Staging.** If there are ten actors who can play the role, but one has deliberate, simple, suspenseful staging in her monologue—while the rest either wander or freeze in place because they have no choices—who is going to get the part?

- **Preparation.** If there are ten actors who can play the role, but one is solidly prepared—while the others are totally thrown if they go up or hesitate on a line or two[8]—who is going to get the part?

- **Acting.** If there are ten actors who can play the role, but one has made her intention intensely personal, and is investing her whole heart in her performance—while the rest are trying to "do well"—who is going to get the part?

---

8   I actually think that overall, actors get too obsessed with lines at auditions. It's not about whether you lose a line or not—*everyone* loses lines, and you will go up sometimes. The point is, how much are you *thrown* by going up? Can you incorporate the "mistake" into your performance instead of condemning your whole audition or trying to start over? There are actors who lose lines all the time, but never let us know about it. Even if an actor has obviously lost a line, we find out a lot about her when we see how she handles it. When you lose lines, *stay in.* Breathe, have that moment—as *part* of your story—and calmly figure out what you need to do (jump ahead, paraphrase, make something up) to keep the story going. When you go up on lines in rehearsal, welcome the unexpected opportunity to practice this! After it happens to you, go back to the text and drill that section so it will be less likely to happen again.

- **Audition technique.** If there are ten actors who can play the role, but one is at ease in the room, looks like he *loves* acting and seems great to work with, who is going to get the part?

- **Research.** If there are ten actors who can play the role, but one happens to have thoroughly researched the play, the playwright, the theater, the casting directors, and the director, so that she can chat knowledgeably if the opportunity arises, who is going to get the part?

- **Material choice.** If there are ten actors who can play the role, but one has an excellent, relevant, specifically-chosen piece the auditors have rarely or never seen before, and that he is excited about performing—while the others are doing pieces from the 1980's that the auditors have seen hundreds of times—who is going to get the part?

Veteran New York stage actor Peter Maloney says, "If they don't cast me, I want it to be their fault, not mine."

Beyond the act of auditioning, notice that the qualities above also speak to being someone of great character, who takes pride in doing the best, most complete work possible. That actor is going to be primed to excel in whatever she is cast in.

Raising your percentages means you are systematically taking ownership of each part of your auditioning process. It also means constantly maintaining and developing your artistic skills.

If you can consistently walk in the door with *all* of the above qualities in place, you will be raising your own percentages to the scary but exhilarating place of having done everything in your control that you can do.

Then it's up to *them*—and countless factors that are totally out of your control—and you can go on to the next audition.

About "Them"

These are some thoughts from behind the audition table.

My first piece of advice is to become an auditor—one of "Them"—if you possibly can, even for a day. Watching other actors interact and perform under pressure is guaranteed to inform the way you audition. You will see actors who are confident, actors who sabotage themselves, and actors who just try to get it over with. You will understand how often everyone behind the table roots for an actor and wants her to be good. And, you will get a perspective you can't get any other way on how much material choice impacts auditions.

I routinely ask actors in my classes if they've ever watched monologue auditions. The ones who have, even if it was just for one round of auditions, give almost exactly the same answers as very experienced auditors when I ask:

- How many of the actors who auditioned looked happy to be there? The consistent answer: 10% or less.

- How many seemed to like performing their monologues? The consistent answer: 10% or less.

- How many of the monologues were about negative topics played negatively?[9] The consistent answer: About 80%.

---

9   I will also discuss negative monologues in "What Might Not Make a Good Monologue," and "The 'Hello, this is me' Monologue."

- How many of the actors had staging for their monologues—clear and specific choices of movement? The consistent answer: Few to none.

- What was it like to see actors whose material choice was not what was asked for, or that worked against them? The consistent answer: Uncomfortable/bad for the actor.

- What was it like to see the actors who looked happy to be there, who had clear choices, great material, and seemed to enjoy acting their monologues? The consistent answer: A huge relief.

- Were you surprised by the realization that auditions *aren't personal*? The consistent answer: Yes!

When considering material choice from the point of view of the auditors—"Them"—I find it necessary to also talk about overall audition technique. This is because the presence or absence of good audition technique always greatly affects how any choice of material is received. Following is what I wish all actors knew going into the audition room.

They Are On Your Side

They really do want you to do your best. Their interests and yours are the same, which is that you give them positive reasons to work with you, now or in the future. When we do rounds of mock auditions for the final class of my monologue workshop, actors consistently say they realized they truly were rooting for everyone they saw. Though seasoned auditors might show less enthusiasm because of their amount of experience, it really is true: we want the actor to have a good time and we want to have a good time. We want something positive to come out of each audition.

They Really Want You to Bring In What They Asked For

The first way to end their being on your side is to announce that you're doing a monologue whose style, period, or length is other than what they have requested for the audition.

They Appreciate Warmth and Good Manners

Actors with strong audition technique frame their material and performance positively and attractively. The best thing you can show when you walk in the door is they can sit back and relax and not have to worry about you. Rise to auditions the way you would rise to hosting an event that is very important to you. Make eye contact, smile, and communicate that you have it all under control. Translate nerves into excitement. Breathe, and do one thing at a time. Thank them sincerely at the end of the audition—it's your curtain call—and go on to the next one.

They Have Seen it All

If you watch a few days of auditions, you'll see it all too. The purpose is not to try to blow their minds with the most amazing audition they've ever seen. It's to give them a *taste* of what you can do as an actor—or a taste of what you could do with the part. It's to showcase your preparation, your focus, your ability to commit to choices and tell a clear story, and a positive sense of what it's like to work with you. Anything veering out of these areas such as too-familiar behavior, material choices that don't make any sense given the audition's purpose, or over-the-top interpretations, can make you look green, out of touch, or like you live in Crazyland.

Show Them What They Need to See

Your carefully considered research should guide you in choosing the monologues that *help* them imagine you in their show, company, school, ensemble, or clientele. Thinking from the auditors' point of view in this way is what I find lacking in many auditions. Stop asking yourself, "What will make them like me?" Ask instead, "What would *I* need and want to see if I were holding this audition?"

Don't Go In To Suffer

Above I mention the statistic of actors doing "negative monologues played negatively." Many, if not most, monologues *are* about a character having a difficulty of some kind, but that's not what I mean by negative. Rather, I mean monologues that substitute cynicism, anger, or depressing subject matter for real drama. In addition to this, even in wonderfully written monologues about difficult problems, actors often have a tendency to act them *for* the problem—and the accompanying negative emotions—rather than for the *solution*.

If you multiply this tendency by about 80% of the number of actors seen in a day of auditions, this might be the reason your auditors appear a bit shut down when you enter the room. They are depressed! They have just seen a string of characters suffering, raging, and lamenting their abusive father, their recent abortion, their devastating breakup, or the end of the world—with no glimmer of hope or heroism in the bunch.

I'm not saying you shouldn't do a good monologue about a negative subject for the right audition. I'm not saying you should only do happy material, or that you should impose an inappropriately cheerful tone on a somber monologue. I'm saying that an actor must attempt to show his character *facing* the problem, as opposed to complaining about it. Then you have a chance of giving your audience something, instead of bringing them down with you.

The great Shakespearean director and teacher John Barton says that even the direst of Shakespeare's soliloquies must be played to show the character trying to *handle* his predicament—and the accompanying rage, terror, or confusion. He warns actors about falling into the trap of only playing what the character is *feeling,* as opposed to what he is trying to *do.* I think his advice applies to all monologues (and to all acting, for that matter).

Never Take Their Responses Personally

I often quote the statistics that when it comes to saying hello and interacting in the room, 10% of actors look happy to be in the room; 20% clearly look unhappy, and the rest are just sort of neutral—which is also not happy. I think this is probably true of auditors too. Part of it is because it can be exhausting to sit in auditions, part of it is because it is hard to smile at someone who is not smiling back at you, and part of it is for reasons you will never know about.

Instead of taking the auditors' neutrality or seeming coldness personally, play what you want, which is for them to know that you are absolutely *fine,* no matter how they may or may not respond to you.

For the small percentage of auditors who are actually and actively rude or mean to the actors they see, know this: something happened to them in their life that made them capable of treating you this way that has nothing to do with you. Some dream they had got shattered, and now they are compelled to take it out on those who are still hopefully pursuing their own dreams. All you can do is know this, silently send them sympathy, and go on your way.

Don't Go In to Get—Only Go In to Give

I remember David Mamet telling us, "Good actors are generous." Trying to get something from the auditors—a sign that they liked you, your material, or your performance—will always backfire. Even if you are subtle about trying to get their approval, they will sense it—and that will work against you. They are under pressure. They need to make the right choices for their project. Help them do this by not asking for anything in the room. Instead, *give* them things: a sincere and positive hello, the best performance you can muster, an easy transition out of your acting into any chatting that may or may not happen, and a positive thank you and exit. They will appreciate you for it.

Have 20 Monologues

This is the secret weapon that will help you deal with any problems that auditors may have with your material choice. Throughout this book I'll talk about the importance of doing research on each audition to help guide your choices. In the end though, there's no way to know their taste or preferences with 100% certainty. Occasionally I'll even hear about auditors being short with actors concerning their material choices, saying things like, "I don't see you in that role." Or, "Well, that's the 25th time I've seen *that* monologue this weekend." Your best recourse is to be able to smile calmly and say, "No problem, I've got nineteen others—what would you like to see?"

Research Every Audition

"What kind of monologue is right for me?" is an unanswerable question, because it leaves out…

- For which project?

- For which director?

- At which theater?

- For which school?

- For which casting director?

…or any number of similar questions that need to be answered before the best monologue for *that* audition can be decided upon.

For every audition you do, you should actively research any school, theater, or individual you are going to be in front of.

Sometimes you will find out a lot of information, sometimes you will hear contradictory information, and sometimes you will find little or no information. It's about being willing to do more than the next guy, even when there is not always an immediate payoff. Doing your research diligently will make you into an infinitely more knowledgeable and savvy auditioning actor over a period of time.

Thanks to the internet, there are more resources than ever before when it comes to researching auditions. You can also ask other actors, or any industry professionals or teachers you have relationships with. Also, don't forget the many actor chat rooms online.

Are you always going to find a monologue that addresses *every* facet of the research you do? Of course not, but doing the research will help define the worlds you are entering and interacting with when you audition. Research will help narrow your choices and give you information that may help you raise your percentages.

Also, anything you can do to identify your auditors as individual people and artists—instead of a nameless "Them"—will empower you, and will change the way you walk into the room. Try it. Use the considerations below to do complete research on your next audition and see how it changes your experience.

What should you research?

Research the Audition Requirements

The first place to start your research is the audition notice. Note anything the auditors have requested regarding length, period and style. Make it a point of professional pride that you always follow audition requirements to the letter.

This may sound harsh, but it's true: there's nothing that says, "I am undirectable and I don't listen" like an actor who brings in a three-minute contemporary piece to an audition that requests a two-minute classical monologue.

It is easy to approximate the requirements, or to become convinced that exceptions should be made because of your love of or rightness for the piece, or the way that you act it, or because you've run out of time and just don't have anything else. These practices are the marks of amateurs.

Bringing in what they've asked for is the first way you show that you listen and that you respect their needs. See requirements as artistic challenges rather than limitations, and get creative and resourceful about how you meet them.

Research the Project

When auditioning for a role, for different reasons you may or may not choose to do a monologue from the actual play being cast. (This will be discussed at length in "Auditions for Stage Roles.") Regardless, you can certainly immerse yourself in the world you will be entering with your audition for that play.

Use your auditions for specific plays as the perfect opportunity to study the play itself, the playwright, the genre, and any accompanying historical or cultural references you will need to know about. Doing this for every such audition can be enriching in and of itself, and will pay off in future auditions and productions.

Research Schools

If you're auditioning for graduate schools, undergraduate acting programs, or any kind of acting training, research the biographies of the faculty, the school's training philosophy, and the playwrights and directors of past student productions. If the school is affiliated with a professional theater (such as the American Repertory Theatre at Harvard, the Old Globe in San Diego, or the Atlantic Theater Company or Playwrights Horizons in New York), research that theater's mission statements and past productions too. It is also helpful if you can find out what material past successful auditions for their programs have consisted of—not to copy, of course, but to give you a sense of what the admissions auditors respond to.

Research Theaters

If you're auditioning for a particular theater company, or its intern or apprentice program, definitely note what has been chosen for the upcoming season, and also the past productions of that theater. It can be a very good choice to bring in a piece by a playwright the theater has produced or will be producing.

Or, to do monologues in a style or genre the theater often produces.

Look on the internet for the theater's mission statement. It is not advisable to do a Sam Shepard monologue for a theater whose mission is to produce the newest international plays, like New York's The Play Company. Instead, this general audition would be a wonderful opportunity to research non-American playwrights you respond to.

The mission statement can not only point you in the right direction, but also help you to avoid inappropriate material. For example, Carl Forsman, artistic director of New York's Keen Company (and now also of the Dorset Theatre Festival), spoke about his experiences with actors doing inappropriate material for his EPAs[10] when we interviewed him for *The Monologue Audition Video (DVD)*. He tells how, "Almost without fail, someone will come in and do a monologue describing how they raped someone."

Well, here is Keen Company's mission statement—which anyone can find on the internet. Read this and decide whether a monologue about raping someone would be appropriate to bring to the Keen EPAs.

> *"Keen Company produces sincere plays. We believe that theater is at its most powerful when texts and productions are generous in spirit and provoke identification. Inspired by the works of early 20th Century American playwrights, Keen Company demonstrates that an earnest intent can still be sophisticated. We are unafraid of emotional candor, vulnerability, and optimism. Keen Company seeks to create a culture of artists, technicians, administrators and audiences who share a desire to invigorate the theater with productions that connect us through humor, heart and hope."*

---

10   Equity Principal Auditions. These are discussed in the "Choosing Mono-logues" section.

Research Directors

When you know you will be in front of a particular director at a general audition, always look for his bio or résumé, which can often be found online. Doing material you know appeals to that director is always a plus.

I don't suggest that you do monologues from plays that director has directed, but that you get a sense of his past productions, tastes, and preferences, and bring in material that you think will interest him. Carl Forsman says that he always pays more attention when an actor brings in a monologue from an early 20th-century American writer, such as Maxwell Anderson. You can gauge this by reading Keen's mission statement, as well as Carl's bio.

Research Agents and Managers

Always do internet searches on agents and managers before you meet them, and ask other actors about them. Get to know who the bigger and smaller agencies are, and stay current with which agents are where by reading the *Ross Reports* occasionally. Get good overviews and perspectives on approaching agents, managers and casting directors by reading *How To Be a Working Actor*, *Acting as a Business*, and any other helpful books you can find. (See Resources.)

Research Casting Directors

For film and TV casting directors, find out what they have cast by doing a search on www.imdb.com. Find out if they also cast theater, and research theater casting directors by searching the Internet Broadway Database and the Internet Off-Broadway Database. (See Resources.)

It is very smart to keep a notebook or database of every play and movie you see, and to note the casting directors (as well as the directors).

Knowing which projects casting directors have cast will provide you with context, and possible conversation (if appropriate) when you meet them. It will also help you decide which (if any) casting director meet-and-greets you decide to pay for. If the casting director who cast the amazing independent film you just saw is speaking, it might be worth your time and money to show up.

What Do They Need?

Using the fruits of your research to put yourself in the auditors' shoes and consider what they might be looking for can be very helpful in your material choice:

- A summer stock repertory company might need actors with strong ranges who can work effectively during short rehearsal periods.

- A children's theater production might need a good-natured actor with an extremely high energy level.

- A training program might need students with very good potential to develop, who are extremely focused and dedicated to improving their craft.

- An agent may need actors with great skills and strong work ethics who have a clear sense of how they would most likely be cast right now in most mainstream television, film, and theater productions.

As you can see, the needs of the audition change based on who the auditors are, and what their purpose is in auditioning actors. That's why "What kind of monologue is best for me?" is an incomplete question.

Use Research to Empower Yourself

Research is for *you*. The point is not to go into the room and try to force conversations based on what you've been able to find out about your auditors. Rather, the goal is to become more and more knowledgeable about the business you are entering.

The actor and teacher Cynthia Silver teaches a fantastic acting business class to second-year students in Atlantic's conservatory and NYU programs. One of the first things she does is give students a long list of names from the New York theater community, to see how many of them the students can identify. The names include the casting directors of Atlantic productions. Her point: "If you're in your second year here, you should know who casts the Atlantic mainstages!"

It's easy to have the belief that when you're "ready," you'll get the opportunities and then you'll find out who everyone is. It actually often works the other way: knowing who someone is will help you make sure you get to that audition, and make the most appropriate monologue choices to show them.

Who Are You as an Actor?

I know this can be a daunting question. But pondering the ever-changing answers to it can help you set career goals, and to choose material that will help you move toward those goals.

I sometimes ask actors in my classes (after affirming that they want to work professionally in New York theater), "Can you name your top ten favorite New York theater directors?" (Not just ten, but their ten *favorites*.)

Very few of the actors I've asked can answer this question. I think this is mostly because acting is seen as a difficult profession with few rules, and one in which most actors are expected to be happy if they get cast in *anything*. So why torture yourself by identifying your favorites?

This is why: if you don't know what a goal *is*, how can you move toward it?

The more you know about what inspires, moves, and motivates you, the more targets you will have to aim at. If you find out there's an open call for a play by a fantastic new playwright whose work you just happened to read, you're more likely to get yourself down there than if the name means nothing to you.

Knowing who you are as an actor is a different question than "What is your type?" which is discussed in the next chapter.

It's about knowing what kind of writing, shows, films, and performances make your heart beat faster—the things you saw as a kid that made you want to do this in the first place. It's about knowing which opportunities and auditions you would crawl through broken glass for—and which you can take or leave.

Of course, I'm talking about a career-long, ever-deepening exploration. It's not about putting labels on yourself. I would bet, though, that there are actors you admire who *have* truly defined "what kind of actor they are," with their performance skills, choices of roles, and approaches to their lives and careers. Study them.

Developing and defining what kind of actor you are will make you recognize the opportunities—and the auditions—that will truly help you express that actor. And, it will inspire you in your reading and noting of potential audition material.

Here are some questions to ask yourself. Who or what are your favorite:

- Actors?

- Contemporary plays and playwrights?

- Classical plays and playwrights?

- Theater directors?

- Independent films and directors?

- Studio films and directors?

- Classic films and directors?

- Theater companies?

- Theaters (which stages would you *love* to act on)?

- Styles of acting?

- Types of characters to play?

- Periods in history?

- Cultures?

And some more questions:

- What kinds of stories do you want to tell?

- Who is telling the kinds of stories you would like to tell?

- What do you want to do with your acting? Explore it as a potential career? Support yourself? Support a family? Do certain kinds of projects? Change the world in some way?

- What kinds of experiences do you want to give your audiences?

- What kinds of situations would you love to act in? Broadway tours? Repertory companies? Political theater? Film locations?

- Do you want to be an actor-for-hire?

- Do you want to create your own work?

- What skill levels do you hope to reach as an actor?

- Which actors have reached these levels? How did they do it?

- What parts of your acting do you most want to develop?

- Are you also a writer? A director?

- Do you want to act as part of your community, or do you want to reach the whole world?

- What other questions will help you develop your sense of yourself as an actor?

- What are your acting goals?

It's easy to become so distracted by wanting to get cast and "do well," that you lose sight of what kind of work will actually make you the happiest. Thinking and writing about these questions on a regular basis will give you a deeper sense of yourself as an artist. Then, when you look at the audition listings, you will get a clearer sense of how a particular audition is resonating with who you currently are as an actor, and whether it is for a project you truly want to pursue.

In the beginning of your career, you will probably want to go on a lot of auditions, so that you can practice and build up your auditioning chops. After you have become more experienced, having a sense of who you are as an actor will help you to identify the auditions and projects that will best help you express and develop *that* actor, and move you forward toward your goals.

"Type" Issues

"What type am I?" This can be a very complicated question, especially when you're always finding out more about who you are as an actor *and* as a person. I put "type" in quotes in the title because I don't want to give the impression that I think there's a final answer every actor can arrive at and claim as his casting identity. It's always a combination of you, who is doing the casting, and what the project is.

Instead of fearing being ruled or limited by typecasting, challenge yourself to live in the tension between how people see you and what you know you can do. Very importantly, learn to recognize how the two can overlap. I'm a firm believer in not being limited by rules and trends, but also in knowing what the current rules and trends *are*. That way, you can find ways to work within them, and also recognize the opportunities you have to break them and change them.

When assessing your type in order to choose a monologue for a particular audition, you should consider not only your own personality and physical characteristics, but also the *venue* and the *audience*. Are you aiming at prime time television? Community theater? The monologue you choose for your first meeting with a television casting director will likely be different from your audition piece for an avant-garde theater company. The point is not to pigeonhole yourself, but to be smart about noting the *markets* your auditors are aiming at with their productions or clients.

What Are the Rules for *This* Production?

Ask yourself, "Is this an audition for which I have to acknowledge how I fit into most mainstream casting[11], or do I have some leeway? How much leeway? What might be 'the rules' of the kind of venue or production I am auditioning for?"

The rules change considerably depending on the nature of the production. For example, when casting director Will Cantler spoke at my directing class, he described casting productions of two Shakespeare plays during the same period. One director *only* wanted to see classically trained actors who had studied at the major training programs in this country. The other director wanted to see *no* actors with that kind of background, because he had a different, specific vision of how he wanted to approach the text.

Leads or Character Parts

This is the central question I think most discussions of type come down to: For a given production, in a given market, is the actor in question more suited to a lead or a character role?

Notice I said "for a given production, in a given market." An actor in a small town's casting pool might get a lead he would never be considered for in a larger market. Not necessarily because of his ability, but because of the amount of choice available. In a larger market there will be more actors to choose from, who from the director's point of view might be closer to the role.

Casting is very much an unconscious, dream-like process. Plays and movies are myths and fairytales. There is often an unconscious archetype the writer has envisioned for a role. Sometimes the director has a different idea, and there is also the input and experience of casting directors (whose difficult job it

---

11   If you want to see the general rules of mainstream American casting, watch network television and major motion pictures.

often is to navigate differences in type perception on the part of writers and directors). There is also the input of producers and artistic directors.

Compounding all of these considerations is the fact that type and acting ability are independent of each other. A smart director will fight for the actor who may be a bit less right for the role, but who clearly has superior ability and chops.

These points of view can be very frustrating for an actor to hear about (unless she has directed or cast a project, in which case she will at least understand them). From her point of view, she's an *actor*—so of course she can play the role. But the auditors have to think that not only can she play the role, but that she is the best available actor for the role as *they* see it. And that will never change.

So, an important—though very general—question to ask, and a possible starting place for dealing with issues of type for yourself is, "In *this* production, of *this* story, in *this* market, am I more likely to be seen as the leading man or woman, or as a supporting or character part—the friend, the sister, the co-worker, the villain, the boss, or the rival?"

You can ask yourself the same questions when going on general auditions (whose purpose is to meet actors, as opposed to auditions for a specific part): "Given the market I am entering, *and* the kinds of projects this person directs, casts, or represents clients for, where am I most likely to fall in the casting spectrum?"

I want to emphasize that I am speaking in the broadest of terms. We all love seeing exceptions to mainstream casting practices, such as when a character actor like Paul Giamatti beautifully plays the romantic lead in a movie, as he did in *Sideways*. I think part of that movie's great appeal was that the casting didn't follow many of the patterns we've come to expect.

When you watch a production with the most mainstream typecasting, such as a studio romantic comedy, you will see the lead vs. character part rules followed most closely. Everyone around the lead is usually an easily identifiable type. (And you know an actor is skilled when he can make you care about a broadly written character.)

Casting Exercises

Here are two exercises you can do to understand more about the issues that come up during the casting process.

- Read a well-known play that has several roles in your age range. Pretend that you are the director, and cast the play on paper, using yourself, and also using actors you actually know, or well-known actors. Experiment with how you cast yourself depending on who is playing the other parts. Depending on the play, try casting it both traditionally and non-traditionally—decide how you will deal with matters of appearance, physicality, ethnicity, and even gender. Repeat the exercise with other plays to expand your understanding and insights.

- With one or more friends, read an agreed-upon play that has roles within all of your age ranges. Each of you should then cast the play using each other in some of the roles (but don't cast yourself in your own "production"). In any other parts, cast actors you all know, or well-known actors. Compare the results and discuss the reasons for your choices.

Type and Monologues

In many or most of the auditions you do, you will want to act characters you think *they* think you would actually be cast as. In a meeting with an agent or manager, for example, you will want to use the best of your judgment to show that you are both on the same page about what you can play.

When considering how the type of a particular monologue

fits you, you can ask:

- How am I near or far from this character in:

  » Age?

  » Physical description?

  » Origin (both locale and ethnicity)?

  » Personality?

  » Life experience?

  » Way of speaking?

  » Way of thinking?

- Given the areas in which I'm significantly different from this character, and given my acting, physical, and vocal skills, what will it take to be able to perform the role to a point that is believable for an audition?

- Is this a monologue I should work on for my own development and enjoyment, or a monologue that will serve me in specific auditions? Which specific auditions?

- In what kind of production might I actually be considered for this role?

- Is this the best monologue for me from this play, or is there another character I'm actually more suited for?

A Warning About Typecasting Yourself

If you consider type too rigidly, or try to "type yourself before they type you," you may miss opportunities. There are sometimes exciting exceptions and variations to general casting practices, and situations in which you should strive to be given a shot at particular characters. For example, both Kristen Johnston and Linda Hunt—two completely different actors in appearance and personality—played the same role (Aunt Dan in *Aunt Dan and Lemon* by Wallace Shawn), in professional New York productions many years apart.

One of the most hilarious examples of an against-type monologue in my class happened in 2006. A young woman named Janna Emig, who was in the second year of Atlantic's New York University undergraduate studio, did a monologue she crafted from a transcript of the basketball player Alan Iverson's famous 2005 press conference. In the monologue, Iverson was defending the fact that he had missed a lot of practice. Much of the monologue consisted of repeating the line "We're talking about *practice*" (as opposed to a game). Janna completely took Iverson's point of view, played it absolutely straight and had the class on the floor. She later did it at an all-studio presentation and brought the house down.

Janna could not look or sound less like Alan Iverson (and she did not try to imitate him at all), but this choice of monologue showed she had great comic timing, skills with language, and a fantastic deadpan. She demonstrated the kind of abilities seen on the best Saturday Night Live sketches. Should she do that piece as her "Hello, this is me" monologue, or at auditions featuring traditional or mainstream casting? Absolutely not, but there are definitely opportunities for her to use it, such as auditions for sketch comedy shows and ensembles.

Ethnicity

Ethnicity is a factor in casting of all kinds. Again, if you want to see what is currently mainstream, turn on the television and watch movies.

I recently received this question from an actor:

"I often audition with pieces I've done from shows. Being Black, many times the monologues are from African American plays. Does it hurt to audition with these pieces for non-African American productions?"

The short answer: the monologue you do should harmonize with the role that is being cast. The key is to take it case by case. This actor should ask if her material for a particular audition shows that she can meet the demands of the *specific* role being cast, rather than trying to decide a consistent practice for all of her auditions. (See "Auditions for Stage Roles" for a list of qualities to consider when choosing a monologue with which to audition for a specific part.)

I think it's important for all actors to have monologues that acknowledge their predominant characteristics, which include their appearance, playable ethnicity, and personality traits. They should have pieces that show their technical and emotional range.

If they so choose, actors can also have monologues of characters that may not have been written with their ethnicity in mind. For example, I think an Asian American actor has the options to have both Asian American and Asian characters (whose regionalisms and accents she can do) in her monologue repertoire. She can also have pieces that show how she could be cast in not-necessarily-written-as-Asian American contemporary roles, as well as in the classic roles of Western drama.

Writing about this here, I feel the imbalance of how predominantly white most casting is. For example, it's not really practical casting advice to tell white actors that they should have pieces that show what African American, Middle Eastern, or Asian roles they could play, because this kind of "non-traditional" casting rarely if ever happens. But such is the reality.

Accents and Regionalisms

I see a fair number of actors from countries other than the U.S. who want to act here. Aside from solving the legal problems they face in getting paid work, they must also deal with issues of accent—and so must actors who have pronounced American regionalisms.

An actor with a strong accent or regionalism of any kind has two choices:

- Attempt to be cast only in roles that can be played with that accent or regionalism (which of course is up to the opinion of the director or casting director);

- Be willing to work until he can act fully with the completely-mastered accent of his choice.

In my observation, it takes the following to master a new accent as an actor, such as being French, Venezuelan, Jamaican, or Australian and wanting to work in mainstream American TV, film, or theater as an American character with a standard American accent. Some of this also applies to learning any accent.

- If English is a newer language to the actor, issues of vocabulary and comprehension may also apply. This includes expressions and turns of phrase used in everyday language.

- Individual sounds must be learned, including placement of sound in the body and speech articulators.

- Rhythm and emphasis must be learned. In my experience, many actors work on the sounds, but not as many work on the rhythm and emphasis enough to be on their way to a solid standard American accent.

- The actor needs to be able to "find himself" in the new accent. Often, actors feel like they are losing their identity when learning to use good stage speech, or practicing a new accent. If you are working on a new accent, do your best to be playful with expressing more and more of your own self—your power, your vulnerability, your sense of humor—in the accent. Monologues, of course, are an ideal way to practice this.

- The actor must be willing to practice speaking in the accent in her daily life, no matter how silly or insecure she feels. The actor and filmmaker Marianna Palka was an Atlantic student. She is originally from Scotland, and arrived in New York with a pronounced Scottish accent. Using determination, regular drilling of sounds, and most importantly, by forcing herself to use the best American accent she could muster every time she worked waiting on tables, Marianna could speak with an absolutely believable American accent by the end of her first semester.

Play to Your Strengths

I'm the first person to promote monologues as wonderful vehicles for your growth as an actor. Later in this book is a chapter on how to choose monologues that will help you work on acting challenges, build new skills, and expand your casting range.

However, those who audition you only see *this* audition. They never see you in the context of your whole artistic life. They have no way of knowing that your work on a particular monologue has progressed a lot in the last two months—nor would they necessarily care, because they are not in a teacher-student relationship with you. They are in a potential-employer and/or potential-colleague relationship. Even auditors at acting school auditions want to see where you currently are, at your best.

Your auditors only know what they see in the present moment, and whether what they see fits their own needs. Therefore, when choosing material for auditions, you should always take your strengths into account.

I think all auditors will agree that it works against an actor to audition with material she is not yet on top of technically or emotionally.

Most auditors I have talked to say that while they definitely *do* want to see an actor's artistic expression in his monologue performance, and love to see an appropriate level of risk-taking and adventurousness, an audition is *not* a time to stretch—to do something out of your range, or to try a new style or skill you have not yet thoroughly worked on.

Of course, there are always the issues of subjectivity and seizing the moment, and actors have to start somewhere. But your material for specific types of auditions you have time to prepare for should help you show the strongest, most accomplished work you can do within the audition requirements.

Here are foundation qualities I think actors should consistently have very much in their grasp before they start auditioning seriously:[12]

- Truthfulness

- The ability to make specific choices, and to connect to those choices under pressure

- Total preparation—solid on lines, and complete physical choices made throughout the monologue

- Vocal support and clear articulation of language

It can be a tricky challenge to sort out what you want, hope, or intend to do well from what currently are actual strengths that you have. Below are areas that actors may have particular strengths and weaknesses in, for use in your self-assessment.

Before you read them: I *don't* want to place such serious doubts in your head that you prevent yourself from auditioning—we all drive ourselves crazy with self-doubt, and what better place to exercise it than when preparing for a monologue audition?

Rather, the purpose of identifying these categories is so that *over time* you can devise your own ways of assessing when you are ready to begin auditioning with certain kinds of writing and

---

12 Obviously, many of those auditioning for acting programs are hoping to be admitted so that they can *learn* these skills. Aspiring actors who are auditioning for conservatories should work to show the most grounded, connected, honest performances they can, given their previous training and experience.

characters. This can and should include getting the opinions of others whom you trust. These people can include teachers, coaches, other actors, directors, and non-actor friends (but probably not your Mom).

The more specific the questions you ask these people, the clearer and more useful responses you will get back. Ask, "Did I seem to have ease with the language?" "Did I seem fully committed to my objective?" "Could you follow the argument I was making?" "Could you understand all the words?" "Can you see me living in this period?" Not, "Was that good?"

Language Style

All plays are written in a style, it's just that some styles are closer to the way an actor speaks and behaves in his daily life. Which writing styles seem second nature to you? Some actors have a natural affinity for poetic and metaphorical language, such as Shakespeare's, and some run the other way when a verse play is put into their hands. You may feel that Mamet writes the way you already talk, or that you feel most at home speaking the words of playwrights like Adam Rapp, Kia Corthron, Craig Lucas, or Annie Baker. Have you worked until you are at ease with the style of language? When you act the monologue, does it seem to others like the language is natural to you?

Language Demands

Are you up to all of the demands placed on you by the language of the role you are working on? Do you get out of breath when you tackle a brilliantly crafted Shaw argument? How is your speech—can we understand you effortlessly throughout the monologue? Have you mastered the accent? Can you mentally follow the twists, turns, metaphors, and comparisons all the way to the end of the point your character is making in your Shakespeare monologue? Do you understand exactly what you are saying and why you are saying it? Do those watching you understand?

Period

Do we "buy" you in the period? Some actors easily look and feel at home in corsets and waistcoats, and some have to carefully learn how to act with ease within the dress, movement, and behavior codes of other times.

Some actors are naturally a bit formal and have to learn to relax into contemporary roles. Some actors' behavior and speech is *so* casual or contemporary, that unless they put the work in, we really will only buy them in the kinds of roles we see on everyday TV. They don't yet know how to fit into the period, style, and language conventions required by a classical stage role, or by a period television series like *The Tudors*—or *Mad Men*.

Dramatic Range

Along with navigating the period, language, and style of a particular role, are you able to truly expose yourself when playing a character of great softness, delicacy, or vulnerability—such as Romeo, or Alma in *Summer and Smoke*? Can you act as a character of great power and presence—such as Clytemnestra, or Julius Caesar? Can you portray characters who are overpowered by extreme or obsessive emotion—such as Leontes in *A Winter's Tale*, Phaedra, or Electra? These intense roles demand that not only do you understand the character emotionally, but also that you can act with extremely high stakes in a short monologue audition, without losing control of yourself. Like a director or casting director would when casting a role, identify *specifically* how high the stakes are, how much you must commit, and where you need to be willing to "go" to act the monologue effectively. Get feedback on both your commitment and stakes for the monologue.

Comedy

I've met many actors who think they have no comedic skills, and usually they are wrong. They just worry so much about being funny that the real intention of the piece goes out the window.

Most comedy needs to be played totally straight. There is also the necessity though, that while the character can't know what she's saying is funny, the actor *does* innately need to know *why* it's funny. I think it's important to choose comedic material you are truly amused by and that you understand the humor of.

It's extra-important to acknowledge the pace and the rhythm of comedy, i.e., to know not to act Joe Orton like it's Chekhov. You want to get in tune with how quickly the character is thinking. I think all acting needs to be *on* the line, *as* the character is speaking, but in comedy this is make-or-break.

Always remind yourself that every actor has his own strengths and affinities—no one acts all kinds of comedy equally well.

To assess whether a particular comedic monologue is working well enough for you to audition with, first ask *all* of the language and style questions above, and get feedback. Your audiences should be able to see you playing that character. You should be having fun when you act the monologue. And ultimately, most people you perform it for should think it's funny.

In the long term, one of the best things you can do to increase your capacity for playing comedic roles is to study the work of great comedians and comic actors, in all of the periods and styles that interest you.

How to Recognize a Good Monologue

The greatest monologues are unmistakable—when you read one, a whole world opens, and you instantly know you are being told a compelling, hilarious, moving, or fascinating story. Your attention is sustained throughout, and you're never confused or distracted by elements that don't fit. If it's a good part for you, you are eager to work on the monologue as soon as you read it.

I am sure you also often read monologues that don't quite click for you right away. Sometimes this is because the writing is a style you are not familiar with and don't appreciate yet; sometimes you don't immediately relate to the character or circumstances (but you could if you invested some time); and sometimes the monologue doesn't work out of the context of the scene, or because there are flaws in the structure.

I want you to be able to recognize the difference between monologues that might not be accessible to you on first reading—but could be wonderful pieces for you if you worked on them effectively—and monologues that don't work because of problems in the writing.

Don't Trust Monologue Books

You should definitely read some monologue books to look for writers you respond to, and to practice recognizing good monologues. However, being published in a collection does not mean a monologue will work for auditions.

I have just read a recently released collection of monologues from newer plays. I am very happy this collection has been published, because more actors will know about these newer plays and playwrights. Some of the monologues are fantastic and I have already started seeing them in class.

However, about half of the monologues in the book do not work for auditions because of structural or context reasons. Some rely on the audience knowing plot elements (such as the character being very ill) that no one would ever know just by hearing the monologue—so it makes no sense. Some take ages to really get going—there's a lot of hemming and hawing before the monologue really takes off. Some are actually *scenes*—the character is holding one half of a conversation, and answering unheard statements by the other character—instead of monologues. Some change topic completely halfway through (though in some cases, the first half might make a good short monologue). And some make references to things and people that are meaningless out of context.

Nevertheless, I do think it's a great idea to read a lot of these collections so that you can practice your ability to recognize good audition pieces. Here is what you should look for:

- **There should be a strong story structure.** The monologue should have a beginning, middle, climax, and end. Pay particular attention to the climax. Is there at least one clear choice?[13]

---

13   Some monologues have a couple of climax options, and it's important to choose only one in order to focus the build of your story. For examples of this, see my book *The Monologue Audition: A Practical Guide for Actors.*

- **The monologue should tell *one* full story.**
  It shouldn't change subject or focus halfway
  through.

- **The monologue should make sense out of
  context.** (This is if it's from a larger work, like a
  play, movie, or novel.) Your audience should not
  have to know *any* background in order to understand and enjoy the story.

- **The story should get going right away.** If
  you like the monologue but feel there is a lot of
  "leading up" to the real story in the beginning,
  see if starting it a bit later will work. (See "How
  to Cut a Monologue, and When Not To.")

Those context and structural elements must be in place for
any monologue to be in the running as an audition piece. In
addition:

- **You should feel the writing is good.** Here's the
  best way to test the writing of a monologue: have
  other people read it to you, without acting it, so
  you can just focus on the language and the story.
  The story should stand on its own without any
  acting "help." It should be engaging, all by itself.
  Then you'll know you have a good one.

- **The story should affect you.** The monologue
  should be a story you want to tell. You should
  be moved, fascinated, or amused. Your interest
  should be piqued—you should want to explore
  further. Sometimes you won't know for sure
  how you feel about a monologue until you have
  worked on it a bit. If it passes the test for the

qualities above, including your belief that the writing is good, do keep working on it.

- **The role should be a good part for you.** If you're choosing a monologue to audition with, the monologue should be within your age range. You should feel it's a part you can play well, and that others could imagine you in the role.

- **It should be a good monologue for *them*.** When choosing a monologue for a particular audition, it should meet all of the requirements set by those holding the audition. And as a result of your research, you should feel it shows how you might best meet their needs.

What Might Not Make a Good Monologue

On one hand, I believe in complete artistic freedom, and that artists should be able to express anything, anytime, anywhere. On the other, I also believe in being smart about the receptivity of the people you are presenting your work to, especially those you hope will cast you, represent you, or accept you into their training program.

One of the most important qualities you demonstrate with your choice of material is your taste. Another is your awareness of and respect for the requirements of the people holding the audition.

Just like formal attire will make you stick out at a casual party, or grungy clothes will make you conspicuous at a black tie event, so can your choice of material prevent you from harmonizing with the sensibilities and tastes of your auditors.

When you haven't taken the time to do research and to think about your auditors' expectations, you're risking that you'll blow the whole point of the audition, which is for you and them to see how you could possibly work together.

Each of the categories below will have their exceptions. I do believe that the right audition exists for any monologue of quality, but here are some general guidelines about material you might need to avoid at certain auditions.

Age-Inappropriate Monologues

There is often leeway for age difference between the actor and the character in school settings. However, I have had 19-year-old men in my NYU classes want to do a monologue of the character of Dysart, rather than the character of Alan, from the play *Equus* (before *Equus* was once and forever placed on the overdone list). Dysart is the middle-aged psychiatrist trying to reach the teenaged Alan, the afflicted young man in the play.

I think the impulse to do a monologue that is significantly older than the actor might be a holdover from high school, where sixteen-year-olds play Tevye or Mama Rose. It absolutely does not work to do this in anything resembling a professional audition.

Frequently I will have 20-year-olds ask if it is okay to do monologues by characters in their 30's, if the actual age is not clear in the speech. My rule of thumb for this is:

- No, if it's a character that is at all well known, and therefore commonly understood to be of a certain age (like Blanche DuBois in *A Streetcar Named Desire*);

- No, if the character mentions life experiences that, because of age, are hard to imagine the actor having had, such as marriages, executive jobs, or children;

- Yes, if it is a piece that really says something you want to say, by a character that is not well-known, and that does not depend on your being the age of the character in order to be believable for your audience.

Unless you are auditioning for a particular role that is significantly older than all of the actors being considered, such as in a school production, attention should always be paid to age appropriateness.

There is age *range* in casting, especially in theater. I know actors who have played teen roles onstage and in TV and film well into their thirties. And, it is common on stage to have well-known actors playing iconic characters significantly younger than themselves, such as Hedda Gabler or Hamlet. However, you usually have less leeway in an actual audition—there are no supporting factors like makeup and lights. It is important to show auditors that you are realistic about which ages you can truthfully portray. It's also important to recognize when it's time to retire monologues you have become too old for.

If a character's age is not listed or apparent in the script, you can sometimes find out the age range by searching for the original production, and finding out who first played the role. Many professional actors' birthdays are listed on www.imdb.com. Calculate the character's approximate age by figuring out how old the actor was when the play was first performed. (However, do consider the facts that well-known actors are often given age leeway when they are cast in major stage roles, and that celebrities tend to physically be extremely well-maintained!)

Subject-Inappropriate Monologues

A surprisingly large number of monologues are about or contain one or more of the following:

- Extreme violence

- Toilet and other bodily functions

- Sexual explicitness

- "Gross-out" descriptions of various events and practices

Again, one quality an auditioning actor demonstrates is her taste. By no means do I want actors to feel censored in their expression, just to consider that there is a time and a place for everything.

As I have gotten older, I have found my tolerance for many of the above kinds of monologues to be rapidly decreasing. However I do agree, along with most of the other industry professionals in the survey, that artistic validity can sometimes make any of the above topics okay in the right circumstances. For example, well-written comedy can sometimes balance out an off-color topic.

Artistic validity, and the taste of the auditors, can be hard to judge sometimes. You might do fine at an audition held by your peers with a graphic monologue, but not a meeting with a manager who is in her sixties. To help with your assessment of a monologue, put yourself in your auditors' shoes:

- If you heard someone delivering the monologue in real life, would you be intrigued, or put off?

- Considering what the audition is for, and given the differences between you and your auditors, what do you think some of *their* reactions to this monologue's subject matter might be?

Monologues that Wear Out Their Welcome

One rule of showmanship is "Leave them wanting more." An extra, unneeded beat of writing, or two, or three, or four, at the end of a monologue that has already made its point can hurt your overall performance.

You really can tell a complete story and demonstrate some important qualities about yourself in two minutes. Some auditions even ask for one-minute monologues, and it is possible to find effective ones.

Our whole culture has accelerated in the last couple of decades. People are used to processing much more information, including the acting they're watching, in shorter and shorter periods of time. When my generation was starting to audition, the standard was three-minute monologues for auditions. Now, a three-minute monologue can feel endless, even when the performance is strong.

Paying attention to the length of monologue the auditors have asked for is a very testable way of showing them that you're listening, and that you care about their needs and requests.

When an actor ignores length requests, or is unrealistic about how long his monologue actually is, it can appear that he may not be open to direction or being part of an ensemble. It can appear that his attention is on himself and what he feels like doing, instead of on the concerns of those who might cast him.

Make it a point of pride that you never get cut off in an audition because your monologue is too long! To time a monologue, read it out loud at a steady, medium pace, and keep timing it during the rehearsal process—staging and moments found in performance *always* affect length.

Monologues That Are Really Scenes

Sometimes you'll find monologues that are set up as scenes:

> *"How long have you been in town? Really? I didn't know you were here. Can we get together for lunch? How's tomorrow?" (And so on.)*

A monologue that contains reactions to things said by the other character usually doesn't work because the actor is then responsible for creating both sides of the conversation. It's a scene, not a monologue.

With the exception of the *occasional* comedic monologue that builds on this quality cleverly, monologues should be speeches, not interactive scenes between two or more people.

Some audition monologues are written this way, and some have this problem because they have been ineffectively pieced together from a scene. It's fine, however, to piece a monologue together from a scene if you can avoid this problem. (See "How to Cut a Monologue, and When Not To.")

Note: when performing, you *will* always need to work in the moment off of the *perceived* reactions of the other character. Then we are free to imagine what those reactions are, which in a monologue is much more powerful than the dialogue *telling* us what they are.

Confusing Monologues

A number of monologues don't work because they make little or no sense out of context. If you have any doubt, you should try reading the monologue out loud to people who don't know the play, and ask if the story is clear. Symptoms of a monologue not working out of context can include:

- Monologues that mention one or more other characters with no indication of their relationship to the speaker.

- Monologues whose stakes depend on references to events, places, or situations that are not explained, or are not easy to guess about.

- Monologues that suddenly and completely change topic part of the way through (sometimes these types of pieces can be made into one or two shorter monologues).

Overly Negative or Degrading Monologues

It seems to me that so much of what we are seeing on television, in movies, and in some theater is subject matter that is mean-spirited, pessimistic, sensationalistic, degrading, or all four. I think this kind of material gives little to its audience and does little for an actor in the audition room. Unfortunately, these monologues are done frequently in auditions.

I do *not* mean that all monologues should be *happy*. Most monologues are about a character having a difficulty of some kind and this will never change.

I'm talking about the spirit and intent of the writing as opposed to the subject matter. My criticism is of material that *relies* on cynicism, anger or self-pity to tell its story, and usually encourages the actor to stay in these negative states for the duration of the monologue—which believe me, can get really old, really fast.

At the time of this writing I've just had a first class with Atlantic's second year conservatory program. Their assignment was to find a "Hello, this is me" monologue. (See "The 'Hello, This Is Me' Monologue.") Included in the criteria for "Hello, this is me" monologues is that the monologue not be angry, cynical, depressing, or self-pitying. When we heard the class' monologues read out loud, one student who had seen a day of monologue auditions remarked on how much more engaging the "Hello, this is me" material was to hear than many of the negative monologues she'd seen on that day.

There is room for differences in taste and opinion on this issue, and some of the kinds of negative monologues I'm talking about can be perfectly appropriate for specific *roles* you might audition for. I include this observation as something to watch out for, because it really can be so draining to watch a bunch of negative monologues played only for their negativity. Maybe the best question to ask when in doubt is, "What does my audience gain from this monologue?"

Use or Overuse of Profanity

Contemporary playwrights frequently use profanity in monologues. Perhaps this is because many speeches are about a truth coming out for the first time, and often that isn't pretty.

I was trained by teachers who curse like sailors, and profanity in dramatic material doesn't offend me at all. However, some auditors are put off by *excessive* profanity, and there are often guidelines about language for actors in educational settings when it comes to choosing material for school projects and competitions.

If I hear a monologue that has a lot of profanity in it, it will bother me only if I feel the profanity is an attempt to hide a lack of real meaning or content on the writer's part—or being used as a substitute for really committing or revealing himself on the actor's part.

I think the question that can be asked of these monologues is, "Does this profanity really help tell the story?"

Monologues About Acting or Auditioning

Monologues about being an actor can backfire at many kinds of auditions by making you—and sometimes also your auditors—self-conscious about the audition. Acting is about storytelling and transporting your audience. Show them something that defines who you are and what you have to offer apart from the fact that you are an auditioning actor. Everyone else they will *see* that day is an auditioning actor!

Bad Writing

What is bad writing? I think actors should not do writing they feel is trite, general, unintelligent, or condescending to the audience.

I've found that the majority of monologues written only as audition pieces have poor writing. I mean the collections of audition pieces that are not from larger stories (like plays, films, or novels), and that were usually all written by one author.

Occasionally you will find exceptions, but these monologues are usually extremely vague. The comedic ones are often general and broadly written. The serious ones may attempt to create a world, but that world is rarely specific. They are often about pain or tragedy of some kind in an attempt to be dramatic. There is much, much better material out there.

Interestingly, I have found that this criticism most often applies only to monologues written as audition pieces. As discussed in "Monologues from Non-Play Sources," very often a one-time editorial or essay can work wonderfully as an audition piece. This is usually because the writer is speaking from a specific personal impulse, and therefore the subject really matters to him.

Evaluating the quality of a monologue's writing, and carefully considering the other issues discussed in this chapter, will help you avoid material that can work against you. This process will help you narrow your choices for particular auditions, and to pick the best writing you can find.

Your First Monologue Ever

If you have never worked on a monologue before, here are some points to consider when choosing your first piece. You may be searching for a monologue with which to prepare for college or other training program auditions; you may be choosing one for a class; or, you may be working on a monologue just for fun.

If you are planning to audition for drama school, I strongly suggest that if possible, you first work on a couple of monologues just to get experience, before choosing the material you will use in your actual auditions.

I suggest using my book *The Monologue Audition: A Practical Guide for Actors,* and DVD, *The Monologue Audition Video,* as guides to rehearsing your monologues. They will show you step by step how to break down, analyze and stage your monologues, and how to act spontaneously and truthfully without a partner—because most auditors do not want you to act the monologue directly to them. They also show you how to make positive and professional entrances, introductions, and exits.

Though you will need to act your monologue without directly looking at another person, I do recommend that you *always* work with a rehearsal partner. Many actors only practice monologues by themselves, and are then unnerved by having to go into an audition and perform them in front of other people. Having a rehearsal partner with whom you are trading the favor of watching and supporting each other's monologues will allow you both to build confidence in performing.

For my classes, I recommend that the first monologue, for all actors, meet the following criteria:

- You should easily connect to the story and think the monologue has good writing. Therefore, it is probably best if the monologue is from a play, but in my private classes I allow any good-quality writing for the first monologue.

- The character should be close to you in age.

- The monologue should run a little under two minutes when read out loud. A two-minute monologue has a substantial enough length for you to really work on the acting. Later monologues can be shorter pieces, because some auditions request them.

- The language should be contemporary, and close to the way you naturally speak. This way, you won't have to worry about having to apply any additional language or speech skills to make the monologue work. So, no Shakespeare, verse, accents, or dialects at first.

- The monologue should be one that could be performed standing. All monologues can be, unless the circumstances of the story literally prevent it—so make sure the lines of the monologue don't dictate that the character is sitting in a taxi speaking to the driver, confined to a hospital bed or wheelchair, dining in a restaurant, and so on. Your first monologue should support you in engaging your whole body when you act, instead of playing it safe in a chair.

- The monologue should be written to address only one other character, so that you can play to a simple focus point that is centered just behind those watching you, at your eye level.

The "Hello, This Is Me" Monologue

I have come to define this kind of monologue during the past few years, after hearing repeatedly from experienced auditors that some monologues actually make it difficult to get to know an actor and what he can do. Here are comments from two of the industry professionals we interviewed in *The Monologue Audition Video:*

> *"They want to make that good impression, they want to do it bigger and better than whoever was in the room before them—and so they do too much."*
> —Todd Thaler, Casting Director

> *"I'd much rather see something that shows a smaller range, that is very clear, and carefully prepared, and thoughtfully done—than something that's all over the map."*[14]
> —Christian Parker, Associate Artistic Director, Atlantic Theater Company

Trying to show everything you can do in one audition is like wearing all of your nice dresses to a party.

---

14 Doesn't Christian's description make you want to do a monologue?

I think it can be a very freeing realization that you don't have to represent every facet of your range in one audition—and that you can actually hurt your chances if you try to. I developed the idea of the "Hello, this is me" monologue in response to this issue.

A "Hello, this is me" monologue is a "handshake" monologue that helps you make an effective first impression. It shows you can act simply and truthfully under pressure. It is close to you in personality, language, and behavior. It harmonizes with an essential part of who you are. It doesn't have any qualities that distract from your acting, or from getting a distinct sense of *you*. Instead of an attempt to show everything you can do, it's an *invitation* to see you do more.

A great "Hello this is me" is a wonderfully comforting, empowering monologue to have in your repertoire. It fits you like a glove and gives anyone who sees it an engaging first experience of you. Once you find it and rehearse it, it's always in your back pocket—you can do it at a moment's notice.

Qualities of the "Hello, This Is Me" Monologue

A "Hello, this is me" monologue *should* be:

- Very safely within your common sense playing range. No one should have to stretch *at all* to imagine you in the part.

- Contemporary. It should be from a time period close to now, or extremely accessible in content and language. There should be no period references that will date the character and story.

- Personal. It should be about a topic you connect to, care about, and want to express.

- Good writing. The monologue should have a solid story with a clear beginning, middle, climax,

and end—and it should be ~~pleasant~~ to say and to
listen to.   *is people are trying to find*
hope in their monologues.

- From a ~~play,~~ if the audition is for theater. I think
  it's a great practice to routinely notice which
  characters and monologues in plays are *your*
  "Hello, this is me's." For some auditions, you
  can do non-play material. Ultimately, I suggest
  having a handful of "Hello, this is me's" from
  different sources.

- 90 to 120 seconds in length—or exactly observe
  the length specified by the auditors.

- Material you do well and that you feel ~~ready~~ to
  audition with.

So far, these are pretty much the qualities of any good audition monologue. The "Hello, this is me" monologue is actually
more defined by what it *isn't*.

The "Hello, this is me" monologue ~~should not~~:

- Be a character far-removed from you in age or
  type.

- Require an accent other than the one you speak
  in, or are ordinarily cast in.

- Have highly stylized or complicated language.

- Be about any shocking, graphic or overly inti-
  mate, "too much information" sort of topic. (See
  "What Might Not Make a Good Monologue.")
  Just as there are inappropriate things to say and
  do at a job interview, when chatting with a new
  acquaintance at a social or business function, or

even on a first date, there are subjects that your monologue choices should avoid at a general, or meet-and-greet type of audition.

- Have any other quality that's easy to hide behind, like excessive jokiness, profanity or sarcasm.

- Be written by you, in most cases. I don't think an actor should necessarily do a self-written monologue for a "Hello, this is me" because of its potential to make her self-conscious. (See "Self-Written Monologues.")

- Be overdone. (See "About Overdone Monologues.")

- Attempt to show multiple facets of your range.

- Be intensely dramatic (like Medea).

- Make you so emotional that you are likely to break down in the audition.

- Be a challenge or a "stretch" for you. The audition is challenging enough! The monologue should be something you do well within your existing range. (See "Play to Your Strengths.")

- Be about someone else. Some monologues are devoted to describing or complaining about another person. The purpose of a "Hello, this is me" monologue is that we get to know *you*.

- Be about acting or auditioning! A "Hello, this is me" should not be about wanting to be an actor, or to be famous. Consider how many actors an

agent or casting director encounters on a daily—
or hourly—basis who are dying to be stars. It's
old news. Show them *you*, of which there is only
one.

- Here's the big one: it should not be negative.
This includes angry, cynical, sarcastic, self-pitying,
self-hating, depressing, or neurotic. In short:
don't go in to suffer. Comedy can sometimes
take the edge off some of these qualities, but be
very careful.

- Along with this last one, my number one no-no
for women: it should not be a piece about a man
treating you badly. Isn't it amazing how many
of those monologues are out there? It's time to
move on.

As you can see, the "should not's" really define this kind
of monologue, because they take away many of the places that
actors go to "be dramatic." Observing the "should not's"
will keep you from doing many of the things industry people
complain about.

It might seem like I've eliminated basically all of your subject
choices, but I haven't.

It's *great* to have any of the following qualities in your "Hello,
this is me" monologue:

- Vulnerability (but not to the point of collapsing
in tears). I think all great acting is vulnerable in
some way. It's not compelling to watch someone
who knows everything. We always love seeing
an actor take the risk of revealing a little bit of
himself.

- Fascination

- Wonder

- Pondering something important to you

- Passion

- Romance

- Hope

- Humor

The best way to test a potential "Hello, this is me" monologue is to ask yourself, as you would with any monologue whose appropriateness you're testing, "If someone came up to me at a party and started speaking this monologue to me, would I be interested in knowing more about that person? Or, would I be put off by their anger, suffering, or bitterness? Would I be intrigued, or would I feel like it's 'too much information'—too personal of a conversation to have with someone I've just met?"

When to Do a "Hello, This Is Me" Monologue
A "Hello, this is me" monologue is good for the following kinds of auditions:

- A first meeting with an agent or manager

- A first meeting with a casting director

- A theater's general auditions (for which the purpose is to meet actors, not to cast particular roles)

- For a training program, if paired with another piece that does show range. (See "Choosing Contrasting Monologues.")

Unlike auditions that are for a particular role or season, the purpose of these meet-and-greet auditions is to get the *beginning* of a sense of what you're like as an actor. If you've made a positive impression as an actor and as a person, and if you're somewhere within the spectrum of what the agent, casting director, manager, or theater is looking for now or in the future, the relationship can progress.

It's Worth the Search

Last year, for the first time, I made the "Hello, this is me" monologue the first assignment for my New York University undergraduate second year class at Atlantic. I gave them the above requirements about what to look for and what to avoid. I required the monologues to be from plays, but *not* to be on the overdone lists. They had about six weeks over a semester break to search for monologues and make their choices.

Just a few students found great pieces right away. Many of the others went a bit crazy looking for their "Hello, this is me" monologues. Those who started late suffered the most, and lost some sleep. Some pleaded for exceptions in the length or subject matter rules. I was strict about the length so that they would learn to truly listen to the requirements of an audition and make it their habit to always meet them. They were not allowed to complain about the search, because in my opinion, any actor who complains about having to read plays to find a great audition piece is in the wrong business.

Many of the group went through four, five, or six choices before finding a fantastic "Hello, this is me." But lots of the rejected monologues were great choices for other kinds of auditions, so these actors were already starting to build a repertoire from their searches.

I hoped to get this group to break through their initial resistance to doing what it takes to find the absolute best audition material. That resistance always comes down to procrastinating about reading.

I was thrilled that most of these students found great "Hello, this is me's," many of which I had never seen before. These are monologues that they can just walk into an agent's office or a general audition and do, that are not seen a lot, and that really help their personalities shine.

When we discussed the assignment, many of the group said their perspective changed from believing that a good monologue is hard to find, to being amazed at how much great writing is out there. They said they now realize how many writers they don't know, and are inspired to read regularly and often. They were also excited to do the pieces they found along the way that just weren't quite right for this particular assignment. Searching for a monologue with such defined requirements broke the ice, and for the rest of the semester, finding a monologue was not an issue.

When Should a Monologue Be from a Play?

There are definite trends, but not every audition will have hard and fast rules about whether monologues should be from plays. The following types of auditions will *tend* to want the material choice to be from plays:

- Training programs

- General auditions for theaters

- EPAs (Equity Principal Auditions)

- Auditions for roles in plays

- General auditions for casting directors who mostly cast theater

- Summer stock

- Repertory theaters

- The monologue portion of musical theater auditions

- Intern or apprentice programs at theaters

The following types of auditors will be more likely to accept your doing well-written monologues from non-play sources, but you should have monologues from plays ready to do if requested:

- Agents

- Managers

- Casting directors who mainly cast film and television

- Theater companies or directors who create work from found sources or real-life stories

- Film directors

When in doubt, ask. Try to find out before the audition if doing a non-play monologue is acceptable.

If you can't find out, and if you have a non-play piece that you feel is well-written and particularly right for the audition, you can simply and politely ask in the audition room: "Is it all right if I do a monologue that is not from a play? I have a piece I'd love to show you that I think is great for this audition. If not, I also have one that is from [title of play]."

Classical, Contemporary and In-Between

"Please prepare two monologues: one classical, and one contemporary." These are the instructions many aspiring actors strive to fulfill for the first auditions of their lives—to get into acting school. Sometimes the schools are explicit about what they define as classical and contemporary, and sometimes they are not.

What Is a Classical Monologue?

The Juilliard School's website gives the most specific definition of classical monologues I have seen, and I think it's a good starting point:

> "Greek plays in verse[15] translation, Lope de Vega, William Shakespeare, Christopher Marlowe, John Webster, John Ford, Racine in verse translation, William Congreve, and Richard Brinsley Sheridan."

---

15 If you are applying to graduate or conservatory acting programs, it's important to know that most of them prefer and/or expect your classical monologue to be written in verse.

This means Juilliard defines "classical" as starting with ancient Greek drama, and continuing through the beginning of the 19th century.

Obviously, this is not a complete listing of the writers of these historical periods.[16] Reading the writers who were contemporaries of the above playwrights will be an enriching and fruitful part of your ongoing monologue search.

What Is a Contemporary Monologue?

Well, first of all it depends on who is asking for the contemporary monologue.

Some auditors mean plays of the last ten years when they say contemporary. Juilliard accepts any monologue from Chekhov onward as contemporary.

Monologues from plays written in the 1970's and earlier still tend to qualify as contemporary in some types of auditions, though in addition to being overdone, many have become dated. You are going to stand out in most auditions that ask for "one contemporary monologue" when you do good monologues from plays of the last five to ten years.

Strong opinion: I think it's especially important for young actors to do newer plays whenever possible and appropriate. Young actors should be recognizing the writers of their own generation, and speaking with their monologue choices about who they are as actors and as human beings in *this* world, as opposed to the world of twenty or thirty years ago.

This is another area in which your research will pay off. If you can, find out what your auditors define as "contemporary." If you can't, study all of the other factors of the audition to decide which specific time period will be most appropriate. For reasons discussed later in "About Overdone Monologues," you should usually stay away from the most-known American plays of the 1960's—1990's (unless of course, an often-done monologue is requested).

---

16 But, if you are preparing an audition for Juilliard, I would stick to these writers, since they are named so specifically!

There is also the possibility at some auditions to do contemporary monologues that are not from plays. (See "Monologues from Non-Play Sources.")

Classic vs. Classical

Even if we decide to define contemporary drama as being of the last fifty years, and classical drama as early 19th-century and earlier, there is clearly a huge amount of playwriting being left out that is considered "classic." The playwrights include some of the greatest names in Western drama.

So, when should you do your monologues by Shaw, Wilde, or Pirandello? Is there a place for absurdist audition pieces by Ionesco, Beckett, or Genet? When should you do Brecht?

The answers lie in the auditions themselves. Consider the purpose of an audition and what might be most important to show the auditors. You can do a monologue written by:

- George Bernard Shaw for a theater that has produced his plays and plays of his time;

- Eugene Ionesco, Jean Genet, or Samuel Beckett for a general audition at a theater that regularly produces absurdist or avant-garde work;

- Arthur Miller, Eugene O'Neill, Bertolt Brecht, Herik Ibsen, August Strindberg, or Anton Chekhov as a contrast piece to your very contemporary "Hello, this is me" for an audition that requests two contrasting monologues, or for a training program that does not specify wanting to see classical pieces.

But Aren't a Lot of These Monologues Overdone?

Yes, many of them are. At this point, I would discourage a young woman from doing Nina's monologue at the end of Chekhov's *The Seagull*, because it has been done *so* often, and particularly because she talks about feeling like a bad actor—I don't think anyone should saddle herself with having to say that at an audition. I would discourage young men from auditioning with any of Tom's monologues from Tennessee Williams' *The Glass Menagerie*. Those are honestly *the* two classic characters that, in my experience, stand out as not needing to be auditioned with again anytime soon. And I'm sure other auditors would name a few other classic monologues they've seen too many times.

However, the amazing plays and characters of these great 20th-century writers are classics that have stood the test of time and will always be with us. Working on them, and learning to do them well, is an invaluable part of your acting life. I think you should work on the ones you love and feel you fit best, and have them ready to go for the right auditions. So later on when discussing repertoire, I will suggest that you survey these great plays to explore which roles are closest to you.

There is also the possibility, in many cases, of finding lesser-known characters by great writers. For example, instead of doing Blanche from *A Streetcar Named Desire,* or Maggie from *Cat on a Hot Tin Roof,* look to Tennessee Williams' lesser-known full-length plays, and shorter works.

Choosing Contrasting Monologues

The contrast request is a direct invitation from the auditors to show some of your range. However, don't go overboard and try to show the outer reaches with each monologue. A good strategy is to choose one monologue that's close to you, such as a strong "Hello, this is me." The second piece should show range in a specific direction that is an asset of yours.

When auditors request "two contrasting monologues," or "one classical, and one contemporary monologue," it's almost always expected that one piece will be comedic and the other dramatic. At the very least, auditors will expect the monologues to contrast in mood or tone.

If an audition request for two contrasting monologues does not specify period, assume contemporary. But in this case, since they did not specify, and depending on what the audition is for, you might expand the definition of "contemporary" for one of the pieces to include early to mid-20th century writers. If the translation is good and non-stuffy to hear and speak, it could even be Chekhov, Strindberg, or Ibsen. The other monologue should be one by a very contemporary writer.

Again, when making these choices, the most important question is "What is this audition *for?*" If it's for a theater that has only produced new writing, for instance, both pieces should be relatively new, and the contrast should be in the tone of the monologues and their styles of language.

Choices of Contrast

Depending on what your research tells you would be the best choices for a particular audition, your monologues can contrast in one or more of the following areas:

- Period

- Style

- Complexity of language

- Character type

- Movement demands

- Emotional range

- Mood or tone

- Accent

Make Sure They Contrast Enough

I do occasionally see actors define themselves so narrowly that their two monologues don't show enough contrast. If you have any doubt, ask yourself and others, "In what specific ways are these monologues different from each other? What part of my range does each monologue feature?" If they are not different enough, change one of them.

What If a Monologue Is "Serio-Comic"?

Sometimes it's difficult to classify contemporary monologues as dramatic or comedic. For example, many good pieces start out with humor and end with a definite sense of drama. I would evaluate the overall impact of the piece, particularly the end. Is the payoff pretty serious? You might count this one as a dramatic piece, and make sure there is some definite comedy in your other monologue.

Choosing the Order

Some schools of thought say "Leave them laughing," and others advise to warm your audience up with comedy and then hit them with drama. I don't think either way works every time. It all depends on the monologues themselves, and the experience you have doing them in a particular order. Some considerations:

- If you were following the earlier suggestion of choosing one piece that's close to you, and one that shows range, I think you should start with the piece that is close to you. This way they'll get a clear sense of "you" with which to contrast your range piece.

- Is your dramatic monologue a piece you can confidently "bring home," and feel most steady and grounded doing? Maybe it should be second, so that you're finishing on a note of strength. You can use your starting nerves for your comedic piece.

- Is your comedic piece a nice surprise—a fun and unexpected side of you that rings true in a wonderful way, that you feel confident just jumping into? Then maybe *that* one should come last, and you can use the nerves of starting the audition as high stakes for your dramatic piece.

- You should also take the transition you will have to make between pieces into account.

These considerations are not meant to drive you crazy with indecision. The best way of finding out a good order is to rehearse one combination, and then the other, with a partner. See what each order feels like to you, and get your partner's feedback.

I also can't help talking technique: you should have a clear, confident, well-rehearsed transition between the two pieces, as well as a strong follow-through at the end of each monologue, regardless of which order they are in.

About Overdone Monologues

For a long time, I welcomed actors to work on any monologues they wanted to for my class, because I felt—and still feel—that loving the material is essential to rehearsing a strong audition. Over the last several years however, I've found myself steering students away from the monologues I've seen over and over again. Finally, I started to compile a list of these monologues.

I asked nine colleagues to add to the list, and to take a survey about the monologues we all see the most. I took it too. The survey is featured at www.monologueaudition.com, and the overdone lists are updated periodically.

The colleagues I polled included casting directors, managers, coaches, theater directors, admissions auditors for major under-graduate and graduate acting programs, and those who audition actors for summer apprentice companies. Each of them has seen many thousands of monologue auditions.

We rated over 100 frequently-done, contemporary, mostly American monologues from plays. I also researched the dates the plays were first produced. It was striking to me that so many of the monologues were from well-known plays written in the 1970's and 1980's—the same ones *my* generation did over and over again!

This confirmed that many auditioning actors are not reading as much as they could be, and that they are depending too much on the monologue books. It is a safe bet that if a good monologue is in a monologue book, it is overdone.

If you do an often-done monologue for auditors who have seen many auditions, it is not the worst thing in the world, providing you do the monologue well. But it might not help you avoid the Maybe pile.

An overdone choice won't help you raise your percentages past the large number of other actors who are doing that monologue in an acceptably true and well-acted way. And with the super-overdone monologues, that number is literally in the thousands.

Unfortunately, actors have no way of knowing which monologues are the most overdone, or the least favorite, for a particular auditor. Many monologues are *so* overdone that auditors groan internally, "Oh no, not again!" just at the mention of them.

Out of love for playwrights, let me stress: the vast majority of these monologues are overdone *because they are great*. They've just been used too many times.

I really, really mean it. I made the list because every year, innocent NYU students come to class excited about the fabulous monologues they've found in *Blue Window, The Woolgatherer,* or *Boys' Life*. I don't disagree at all that these are fabulous monologues, but most experienced auditors can literally recite them along with the actor.

An actor who does a good job with a well-written, interesting piece that is something the auditors have rarely or never seen before is virtually guaranteed to be paid more attention than an actor who brings in an overdone piece. Why? Because seeing good new material done well is *entertaining*.

As always, there are some caveats:

- If you are studying monologues in a school setting only, and do not expect to be auditioning for people who have seen a lot of auditions, I don't think you should worry as much about "overdone-ness." However, if you are at all serious about acting, I can't resist urging you to read the most current plays and playwrights.

- A few audition notices I've heard of actually *ask* for often-done monologues so that the quality of the material won't be the issue in the audition. These auditors are reacting to actors who, in an attempt to not do overdone monologues, bring in material that is poorly written. The auditors would rather see a good overdone monologue done well than a terrible monologue that does not serve the actor.

I want you to go for the best of *both* worlds: strive to have wonderfully written monologues that are not overdone.

Ultimately, the only way to prepare for all eventualities is to have many monologues ready to perform. (See "Building Your Repertoire.") Wouldn't it be empowering to have a large enough repertoire—including a few often-done monologues, as well as several lesser-known pieces—so that you'll never be stuck for a choice?

How to Use a Monologue Book

Monologue books have a bad name.

Sometimes, when I ask where they found a particular monologue, actors will sort of guiltily say they found it in a monologue book—perhaps because they think admitting this implies they do not read much.

Monologue books can actually be very helpful guides when you're looking for material you connect to. They are a fast way to experience many different kinds of writers and roles.

The problem is, if you are looking to avoid often-done and overdone monologues, the pieces in those books that appeal the most to you have also likely appealed to thousands of other actors. I've actually heard New York industry people say they can tell when a new monologue book has been released, because they will all of a sudden see the same few pieces—the best ones from the new book—many times in a day of auditions.

I think you should definitely read monologue books because they provide such an efficient exposure to the work of so many writers. However, if you are looking to avoid often-done and overdone monologues, you usually shouldn't do the actual pieces that are in the books, if the books have been in circulation for a while.

I will also repeat my statement from "How to Recognize A Good Monologue" that just because a monologue is in a monologue collection, does not mean that it is a sound monologue to use in auditions. Please see that chapter for discussion of structural and context elements that must be in place for any monologue to be a good audition piece.

There are a few kinds of monologue books:

- **Collections of monologues from the newest contemporary plays.** These are regularly published and you should definitely look at these books and get familiar with the playwrights.

- **Collections of monologues from plays that were written between the 1960's and the 1990's.** These books contain the most overdone contemporary writing. Read them to get a sense of the work of these wonderful playwrights, and for inspiration to explore the lesser-known work of the ones you like most.

- **Collections of Shakespeare monologues.** You can read them to find the speeches and characters you connect to the most, and then read the plays, if you are unfamiliar with them. There are also good online listings of Shakespeare monologues.

- **Collections of non-Shakespeare classical monologues.** These are fantastic resources to help you expand your knowledge of playwrights and plays you can go to for classical pieces.

- **Collections of monologues that are written only as audition monologues, often by one person.** In my experience, with very few exceptions, these collections should be avoided. The writing quality is usually mediocre to terrible. When I read or hear these pieces, it often seems the author's purpose was to make a buck writing audition pieces, as opposed to genuine creative expression. I find the writing usually to be unfunny, vague, undramatic, and unenjoyable to watch. In some of these collections, non-existent "play titles" are listed, and sometimes it even seems the "authors" are made up—actors will search for the scripts and writers only to find they do not exist, or at the very least are not published elsewhere. (To check this, search for the writer and play at www.doollee.com.)

As you read a monologue book, note the pieces you like most, then go to www.doollee.com, where complete works (including lesser known, and short plays) of thousands of playwrights are listed. You will then be able to choose from other plays written by the writers you like most. The website also lists the year a play was first produced—a valuable tool for determining how contemporary the writing is. If a play is available for purchase, there will be links to internet bookstores.

Non-Play Monologues

This chapter contains an overview of monologue sources that are not plays, and some of the ins and outs I have noticed about working with them.

You can do monologues from authored sources such as novels and films, as well as monologues that were spontaneously spoken by someone in real life.

These monologues can help fill some hard-to-find categories, such as comedic monologues for young women that are smart, funny, and non-neurotic.

As with any monologue, your non-play monologue should:

- Have a good structure, including a distinct beginning, middle, climax, and end;

- Be enjoyable both to speak and to hear;

- Be well-written (if by a writer), or well articulated (if from an interview or another "found" source).

Make Sure Your Non-Play Monologue Will Serve You

It can be easy to get carried away with the novelty of doing non-play monologues, especially the more unusual choices such as monologues from blogs, comedy routines, or talk radio. Of course, you should absolutely do any of them you like for fun, or even with the idea of developing theater pieces or one-person shows.

When it comes to auditioning with non-play monologues, think of your audience. Be conscious of what you're showing your auditors and why you're showing it.

Monologues from Movies

I see great monologues in movies all the time. I do think it is important to avoid some of the most famous speeches and characters, because some auditors won't be able to get the original actor out of their heads.

Having said that, I was very moved when a student did one of Jimmy Stewart's monologues from *Mr. Smith Goes to Washington* because the writing was so beautiful and the actor did a great job with the piece. I also just saw a wonderfully creepy monologue delivered by Joseph Cotten in Hitchcock's *Shadow of a Doubt* (Thornton Wilder wrote a lot of the screenplay). I know Mari Lyn Henry and Lynne Rogers, co-authors of *How to Be a Working Actor,* are big fans of monologues from classic films, because so often the writing is top quality.

I have also seen actors do very effective monologues they've adapted from lesser-known characters in more recent films, and from foreign films.

Monologues from Television Shows

Pick the best writing you can, and speeches you are personally very affected or amused by. You should be cautious about choosing well-known characters. Speeches and testimonies on *Law & Order* or other courtroom dramas are usually given by one-time characters, and can be fine choices.

Monologues from Novels and Short Stories

Novels and short stories can be wonderful sources for monologues *if and only if* the author has a good ear for dialogue. Read the potential monologue out loud to others for their feedback, and have others read it to you, before making a choice. Avoid overly descriptive passages. The language should sound active and alive, not "literary."

"Found" Monologues

The monologues from this point onward are even more off the beaten track. I call them "found" monologues. Some examples that students have brought into class:

- In a magazine interview, Mel Brooks muses on what happens to a person immediately after death: "There's a little door you go through..."—hilarious.

- A real-life mafia princess interviewed on *Larry King Live* speaks about life with her father— intriguing and terrifying. A student found this one after I said I wasn't thrilled with a monologue she'd chosen from *The Sopranos*—so she went for the real thing.

- A fashion editor writes about how she re-fell in love with blue jeans—smart, funny, and light.

- A young woman records exactly what she will and will not put up with in a new boyfriend on her blog—outrageously funny.

- One of the first women in space describes seeing Earth from the spaceship—beautiful and fascinating.

- A young Iraqi woman speaks of the treatment she received from her brothers when she became pregnant out of wedlock and how she fought back—horrifying but inspiring.

- In a fake article from the humor newspaper *The Onion*, a disgruntled aspiring fast food employee complains about her job search—a riot.

Monologues from Non-Fiction

Anything by a good writer who is fascinated-to-obsessed with her subject matter is potential monologue material. An actor named Anne Fidler once brought a monologue into class from an old *Betty Crocker Cookbook* about how to throw the perfect dinner party. It was both hilarious and harrowing—there were so many things the hostess had to get perfectly right.

I have also seen humorous, affecting, and moving monologues from memoirs, letters to the editor, and even a slightly spooky page on the internet about how to psychologically prepare for a corporate job interview.

Monologues from Documentaries

Documentaries can be rich and compelling monologue sources. The subject matter tends to be fascinating, and interviewees are often passionate and articulate. One documentary I saw about Jim Jones was packed with gripping monologues by people of all ages and types who had personally known Jones, or been part of his cult.

Monologues from Interviews

Often, your favorite writers, actors, and other public figures are compelling and articulate interview subjects. They may tell a personal story, or muse on a subject they are interested in. The interviews may be published or live. I have seen students do monologues taken from interviews with Orson Welles, Imelda Marcos, Marilyn Monroe, Courtney Love, and many others. See below for my suggestions about how to introduce monologues by famous people.

You can also find monologues in interesting interviews with non-famous individuals. To search online, just type in the name of any topic that interests you, and the word "interview." This will make it more likely that you will find someone actively speaking about the topic, as opposed to an article about it.

There was a very compelling article in the *New York Times* that included an interview with a soldier who had recently returned from Iraq. A student of mine used some simple editing to make the soldier's comments into a very moving monologue.

Monologues from Letters

Another student performed a beautiful monologue taken from a letter written by an early 20th-century woman to the man she would eventually marry. You can find collections of letters written by all kinds of people in every imaginable time and situation. Letters by great playwrights and authors are also fantastic resources and provide a wealth of material apart from their plays and novels and stories.

Monologues from Comedy Writing and Performance

Many comedians have published books of comedy essays and musings, and often these pieces make hilarious monologues. However, sometimes the persona of the comedian is so vivid, it's hard not to think of him as the story is being told. A student of mine did a monologue taken from a Rodney Dangerfield book. Knowing it was Rodney Dangerfield's story tended to upstage the piece. I advised the student to use the piece, which was a very funny account of Rodney's failure with a woman, but not to say Dangerfield wrote it. Instead he should say, "This is a monologue from [title of book]," and leave it at that.

Students have also occasionally brought in monologues taken from standup routines. These can work if an actual story is being told, as opposed to a series of one-liners. The above note about the comedian being well known applies here too.

Monologues from *The Onion* and *"The Best of Craigslist"*

These two sources have provided some of the funniest non-play monologues I have seen recently.

- *The Onion* has endless choices of extremely funny writing that often can be used for audition material. You can read the paper version, browse *The Onion* online, or get any of the many *Onion* books.

- On your local Craigslist.org home page, there is a button that says, "The Best of Craigslist." Click it. You will find numerous rants, essays, and funny or strange postings people have sent in that have been voted as "the best." You have to hunt, but you can find hilarious, impassioned monologues.

Monologues from Blogs

Countless people are blogging and therefore zillions of "monologues" are posted on the internet every day. You'll have to weed through a lot, but if you locate bloggers whose style, wit, and sensibility are close to yours, and who are good writers, you'll often find excerpts you can craft into good monologues.

The Sources Are Endless

In addition to all of the above, I have seen actors do effective monologues from:

- Historical political speeches

- Bridezilla.com

- A phone message left by a Russian real estate agent

- A taped conversation of a Wall Street trader ranting to the London office

- A story told by the actor's own mother, about her childhood

- A diatribe by a caller on talk radio

- A story from the Moth, a revered New York storytelling slam[17]

- An actual funny conversation with the actor's friend about why she would not go on a date with a certain guy

Songs and Poems: Not Always a Good Bet

I really don't think it usually works to do song lyrics as monologues. If we know the song, we will hear the melody in our heads. And even if we don't, the rhyme or the meter often makes the song odd to hear spoken, as opposed to sung.

Similarly, poems, in my experience, only work if they are actually just great monologues, and are not written in rhymed verse.

Cutting and Shaping "Found" Monologues

Some potentially good monologues from found sources need to be cut or even rearranged to work most effectively. Here is what to look for when editing:

- Make sure there is a clear beginning—an engaging opening line. This may mean starting later.

- Make sure your selection stays on topic. If a monologue is from a longer blog, interview, or statement, find one cohesive section.

- Cut phrases that are repetitive, or that do not take us somewhere new.

---

17 See Resources for non-play monologue sources.

- Consider cutting extraneous references—commentary that does not have to do with the main thrust of the speech.

- End the monologue at or just after the climax of the story. If a clear climax is hard to identify, reconsider the choice of material.

- Always read potential monologues out loud to others, and have them read to you, to make sure they make sense and sound good.

Introducing Non-Play Monologues at Auditions

Be simple about introducing these monologues. As I mentioned in the Rodney Dangerfield example above, you don't have to reveal the writer if you feel it would be too distracting.

A student did a monologue from an interview with Marilyn Monroe because she liked what Ms. Monroe had to say, but didn't want to distract from the story by revealing her name. So she said, "This is from a Life Magazine interview in 1962."

Don't be afraid to be honest about the source, though. Hearing it can be intriguing. "This is a monologue from *The Onion*;" "This is from a message left on my voicemail;" "This is from last Sunday's *Times*;" or, "This is from the floor of the New York Stock Exchange."

Monologues with Accents

The subject of accents comes up frequently in monologue auditions. The questions include:

When Can I Play a Character That Has an Accent Other Than My Own?

- When auditors are casting characters with particular accents and regionalisms.

- At a general audition for a theater that often produces plays from a particular region or country. It would be best if it were a two-monologue audition, so that you could do one monologue that has an accent, and one that uses your own accent, or standard American. If it is the first time they are seeing you, and you can only do one monologue, in most cases you should not do a piece that requires an accent.

- For an agent or manager, if it is an accent you have mastered and with which you feel you could be regularly cast. It is also possible, once you are represented, to show your agent or manager a monologue that features a newly-mastered accent.

When Can I Change a Character's Accent?

This is a judgment call. Some monologues work fine without their original accent, and there are some monologues, such as many by Tennessee Williams, that I feel absolutely do not work if not done with their intended accent or regionalism.

On the other hand, Shelagh Stephenson, playwright of the popular play *The Memory of Water*, thinks, and I agree, that it is fine for actors to do many of the monologues in that play without the original English accents, because the characters and the situation in the play (three sisters dealing with their mother's death) are universal. The monologues also happen to be written with very little English slang or turns of phrase.

I would advise against doing any well-known character without the intended accent. I would also advise against doing a monologue that has slang, terms, or references from a specific region or culture unless you are performing it in the intended accent. Doing these monologues without the accents can sound odd and be distracting. If you are in doubt, get the feedback of others about whether the monologue you're considering works without the accent.

When Should Use My Own Accent or Regionalism, and When Should I Speak in Standard American?

Actors with non-American accents or strong American regionalisms often ask this question about auditioning in the United States. The short answer is that you should do monologues that support how you can be currently cast.

If you are confident that you have a good standard American accent, and have received consistent feedback from others that this is so, you should definitely do monologues that feature this skill.

In addition, you should have monologues that work well when performed with your accent or regionalism, because that is also a way you could be cast.

Monologues with Props

I think it's almost always the strongest choice to embrace the theatricality of monologues and therefore avoid props whenever possible. However, there are some prop-dependent monologues that are good enough to be worth the trouble.

Most importantly, props should be as easy to manage as possible. They should emerge quickly and predictably from a pocket or purse, and be easy to put back.

Cell phones have made "on the phone" monologues easy to execute, and these pieces are fine to do in auditions. Just make sure the auditors can see your face and into your eyes as much as possible—there is a tendency to look at the floor a lot during telephone monologues.

Rehearse, rehearse, rehearse. Make the use of props smooth and assured, and be smart about anticipating difficulties. Make turning the cell phone off a ritual (for all auditions) so that it doesn't ring in the room, or in your hands if using it as a prop. Test all props. For example, make sure a letter tears the way you want it to.

Except for the example below, make props look reasonably authentic, such as envelopes with stamps and return addresses, letters written out, or appropriate photographs.

The following should go without saying, but people do it: *never, never, never* have a real weapon such as a knife as a prop, or even a fake gun that looks realistic. I actually heard a casting director describe an audition in which an actor pulled a real knife on her while she was reading with him. He had no intention of hurting her, but she was terrified nonetheless. In a monologue audition, this kind of realism can take the auditors out of the piece. If a gun is absolutely necessary to make the story work, use a colored plastic water pistol that looks completely fake. Your auditors will be able to enjoy the monologue without any worries.

Self-Written Monologues

Actors who are also writers sometimes want to write their own audition material so they will feel more connected to the story they're telling. And sometimes that is the result and the piece works beautifully.

Doing self-written monologues can also backfire, however. Just because an actor wrote something does not guarantee that kind of connection, and if the audition isn't going so well the actor may wonder in the middle of it if the problem is with his acting or with his writing.

If you are an actor/writer, consider the purpose of the audition. Is your self-written piece the best choice? You should get feedback from several people you trust about the monologue's quality and appropriateness.

I also suggest that actors never tell auditors that a monologue is self-written. Knowing an actor wrote his piece can take the auditors' attention away from the acting, because it can be irresistible to evaluate the writing instead of the performance. And, it can be easy to become distracted by wondering if the material is autobiographical.

If you definitely want to audition with a monologue you've written, one trick is to use your maternal grandfather or grandmother's name as the writer's. The author name you use to introduce the monologue will then likely be different from your own, but will be one you feel connected to. Or, you can use another name you feel an affinity for.

"Story" Monologues

I've heard that many auditors think "story" monologues—pieces that describe a past experience of the speaker's—are passive, and should not be used for auditions. These auditors believe that all monologues should address another person directly with a specific request or agenda.

I disagree! (In many cases.)

Depending on the actual story of course, which must be well-written, these monologues can serve actors just as well as any other good monologue if active choices are made about why the character is telling the story *now*.

I think this prejudice against "story" monologue might come from seeing actors perform these types of monologues passively, or perhaps from seeing many badly-written story monologues.

Edmund's seagoing monologue from Eugene O'Neill's *Long Day's Journey Into Night,* and Libby's (sadly, overdone) monologue from Craig Lucas's *Blue Window* are both "story" monologues, but are each pieces of wonderful, active writing.

When considering a story monologue, carefully assess the quality of the writing, and what the character is attempting to *accomplish* by telling the story. You should easily be able to find an active reason for speaking the monologue that you can get behind as an actor.

How to Cut a Monologue (And When Not To)

As discussed earlier, I think it is fine, and often necessary, to freely edit non-play monologues so that you have a clear story and a sound structure.

With monologues from plays, I go case by case. There are many playwrights whose writing I would not touch other than perhaps to begin or end a monologue a line earlier or later.

There are some monologues that can be cut a bit internally so that the story can progress more effectively during the two minutes, or so that the monologue will not exceed the length asked for by the auditors.

All editing should serve the clarity of the story. Reading the possibilities of edits out loud, and having someone else read them to you, will help you hear the strongest choices.

Cut Lines That Delay a Clean Start

I think you should cut all beginning lines that refer to something previously said in the scene that we will never hear about in the audition piece. Very often these lines are actually a finishing up of the last thought before the monologue actually starts. For example, "I see what you mean." Or, "That reminds me of something." We will never know what "that" is.

Sometimes you just need to cut a couple of words that refer to something just said: cut the "I mean" from "I mean, how you can you say I never loved you?" and you get: "How can you say I never loved you?" This is a much stronger opening line.

Other kinds of lines that delay a clean start are "windup" lines like, "I want to tell you something." Or, "Can I ask you a question?" The monologue will have a cleaner, sharper beginning if you cut the windup and just start telling them, or asking them.

Making Internal Cuts

It feels odd to be talking about cutting a playwright's work without the playwright present, but the justification is this: playwrights don't write monologues thinking of the audition room, they write them in the context of a whole scene and play. The reality is that many audition monologues are lightly edited for length, or so that they make sense in an audition context.

An Atlantic student of mine was looking for monologues at New Dramatists, an invaluable New York organization that supports playwrights. (New Dramatists is a rich source of new plays. See Resources.) The playwright of a play my student was reading happened to be there, and he overheard her talking about the play to her friend. They started a conversation, and the playwright ended up editing a monologue for her from his play, himself!

Here the kinds of edits that are possible to make:

- **Cut overly repetitive information**. This is completely case-by-case, and is obviously up to the discretion of the actor. Sometimes repetitiveness works well, and sometimes it holds the story back in an audition context. I have seen many monologues work better for auditions when overly repetitive words, phrases, or repeated use of another character's name are cut. A monologue like this may work beautifully in a scene, but often in the audition room, repetitions chew up time and prevent the monologue from moving forward. If you edit, do it sparingly—sometimes just one or two edits are enough.

- **Cut sections that are complete digressions from the central story.** Sometimes there will be a sentence or a whole chunk of text that meanders off into another direction before the main story of the monologue resumes. If the digression does not aid the story, you might consider cutting it.

- **Cut information that doesn't matter out of context.** Sometimes, halfway through a monologue we will suddenly hear that a new character is present. Or, a reference will be made to someone or something whose significance we have no way of knowing about if we don't know the play. If the story still works without the new information, you should usually just cut it.

- **Add a name for clarity.** This kind of thing happens occasionally: a character in an otherwise effective monologue talks throughout the monologue about "she," but we never find out who "she" is. I think it can be fine in some cases to substitute "Mom," or "my girlfriend," once early on, so that the audience will know what the story is about.

Recognize a Strong Ending

Because monologues usually aren't written for the audition room, it's important to be aware of the moment a complete story has been told. Sometimes monologues will continue past this point, because the beat is shifting in the scene.

Examine the end of each monologue you do, and make a conscious choice about what the last line should be. Sometimes an earlier ending will give the entire speech more impact.

Honor the Writing

I *never* advocate rewriting a monologue or changing a playwright's words just to make the language easier to say or more convenient for the actor. Part of an actor's craft is the ability to make someone else's words her own.

How to Piece Together a Monologue from a Scene

Many auditors recommend not doing this at all, because when the resulting monologue doesn't work, it's usually because the lines still rely on the other character's responses—the monologue is still really a scene.

I think you *can* find great monologues within some scenes if you consider the following:

- Piecing a monologue together works best when the scene in question is already essentially a monologue by one character, with short interjections from the other character that can simply be left out.

- To test a potential monologue of this kind, read your character's lines through as a speech, completely skipping the other character's lines, and make sure it works as a *monologue*—does it have a clear beginning, middle, climax, and end? Are there additional lines by your character that you should cut, so that we don't hear you answering the other character?

- Make sure the monologue builds to a clear climax in the final version, and that your result is a full story—not a collection of fragments.

- Be thorough in testing monologues you piece together from scenes, and get feedback from others about the clarity and strength of the story you're telling.

Auditions for Training Programs and Graduate Schools

The following advice applies to choosing material for graduate, undergraduate, and other training program auditions.

Auditors of all training program auditions want to be shown that an actor is a good fit for their school in sensibility, skill, discipline, philosophy, potential to develop, and eagerness to grow.

Graduate programs will expect applicants to be more accomplished than many undergraduate programs and acting schools will. However, some undergraduate programs are very competitive to get into as well.

One main reason to attend a conservatory training program is to be able to study acting while also studying voice, speech, movement, and other performance classes, which will exponentially enhance the actor's progress. It is therefore important for graduate school auditions, and a plus for other training program auditions, that at least one of your audition monologues clearly gives a sense of how you move on stage, and therefore how at home you are in your body. It's also very good if at least one of the pieces reflects particular strengths in your vocal and language skills.

Note the size of the program to which you are applying, and find out how many actors are accepted into the first year.

Many graduate schools and other smaller multi-year programs are essentially training a group who will become a performance ensemble. They will therefore be paying more attention to type and personality factors in the auditions.

In contrast, for schools that accept large numbers of acting students, type issues are less important, as the focus of these schools will be most intensely on class work—their primary goal is to teach students how to act.

Training programs virtually always publish clear audition requirements. They usually ask for two contrasting monologues (often but not always one contemporary and one classical), and many suggest having additional monologues prepared as backups.

The general wisdom for the two contrasting monologues is to choose one monologue that is fairly close to you, and the let other show some range. (See "Choosing Contrasting Monologues.")

In my opinion, and in the opinions of many of those who watch these auditions, actors should try to avoid the most over-done monologues from the period between the 1960's and 1990's.[18] This is not to say that an excellent performance of an overdone monologue won't be considered, but when you are trying to separate yourself from those around you, having interesting, rarely-seen, well-written material is definitely going to help you stand out. You will be making the statement that you go the extra mile as an actor, and that you are above average in your knowledge of playwrights and plays.

Do consider this, however: when a school such as Juilliard states that it considers writers from Chekhov onward to be contemporary, I think that can partly be taken to mean that the applicant should make sure that the writing of her contemporary piece is top-notch, and that she should not be afraid to bring in monologues from classic 20th-century (as opposed to classical)

---

18   For lists of overdone monologues based on a survey that
     included both undergraduate and graduate school auditors, visit
     www.monologueaudition.com.

plays for her contemporary choice. In other words, she should not sacrifice the writing quality of her contemporary choice for the sake of being different. This is another area in which doing your research and considering the history and aesthetic of the school you are applying to will help you choose pieces specific to a particular institution.

It is important to focus on monologues that play to your strengths. This can be decided with the help of a teacher or coach. You should also have a good awareness of what your personal challenges are—areas you know you need to work on—and you should be ready to discuss them if asked to in the interview portion of the audition.

It is crucial that you know and understand the entire play each monologue is from, and that you are able to discuss the play if asked. You should be able to demonstrate knowledge of the playwright, and to talk about why you chose that monologue.

It is also a mark of a focused and aware actor that you know and can speak articulately about the artistic style and philosophy of the institution if asked why you want to attend the program. Therefore, you can and should find out the production history of the institution, the training philosophy, and the backgrounds of the faculty. You should also make sure through your research that the philosophy and artistic goals of the training program are ones you identify with and want to be a part of.

When auditioning for a program such as New York University's undergraduate drama department, which is associated with several professional studios that students are placed in, take the time to read about each one so that you know the differences between the Stella Adler Conservatory, the Lee Strasberg Institute, Playwrights Horizons Theater School, Atlantic Acting School, CAP 21, the Meisner Studio, and the Experimental Theatre Wing—and so that you can articulate your desire to attend the studio that is your first choice.

As I mentioned earlier, for performance-based programs such as many graduate schools, an actor's physical or personality type can be an important factor, as many schools are essentially "casting" performance ensembles when they audition potential students. They therefore will be unlikely to accept many actors of a similar type. Some of this is out of your control of course, but monologue choice can and should reflect your best opinions of how you are most likely to be cast at that school. For summer programs, and larger college programs and acting schools whose emphasis is more on training than on productions, this is less of a concern, but it is still effective to find monologues that harmonize with your casting range.

I know this is a lot of information to consider! Getting into the top training programs is extremely competitive, and you need to be willing to go the extra mile in all aspects of your preparation.

Doing your research diligently should help you choose the best material for a particular school, while factoring in your own tastes and your sense of who you are as an actor.

I see many actors prepare for graduate school auditions and other training programs each year. It's easy to get obsessed with pleasing the auditors and working hard to get everything right. Giving the audition your best possible shot also means focusing and re-focusing on your love of acting and why you want to do this in the first place. And, it means expressing that love in your material choices, your rehearsals, and your auditions.

I also encourage actors auditioning for training programs, particularly the most competitive ones, not to gauge their self-worth as an actor on whether or not they get accepted. This is because the statistics I have heard the most recently are:

- For a well-known undergraduate program that accepts only eight female and eight male first year students, male applicants had less than a 3% chance of acceptance, and female applicants less than a 1.5% chance (because twice as many women auditioned as men for the same number of spots in this small program).

- For two graduate programs, approximately 1200 actors auditioned for 16 spots. That's less than a 1.5% acceptance rate overall, and the same male to female ratios probably apply. Some graduate programs make a practice of accepting more men, because there are more men's roles in classical plays.

These types of statistics lead me to advise actors who really want conservatory training to be active, not passive, in their approach to applying to schools. Some actors only audition for two or three top programs, to "see what happens." If you are serious about pursuing the best training you can get, I suggest that you:

- **Apply to more than just the most prestigious programs.** Since you are going to be investing a lot of time, effort, and money in preparing for the auditions anyway, research lots of schools and audition for as many that appeal to you as possible. It will give you experience and make your overall auditions stronger.

- **Use this time of intense preparation to enjoy getting better and stronger as an actor.** Invest in your preparation 100% for its own sake. Set achievable goals that are independent of whether or not you are accepted.

- **Get support, and support yourself.** What you are doing is difficult. Build reinforcement from others, rest, and rewards into your training period.

- **Have well-considered plans B, C, and D.** Make alternative plans about training and growing as an actor that you are excited about, in case you are not accepted by your first or second choice programs. Do some research about what other kinds of training are available to you. There are many professional-level training programs and acting schools that are not college degree programs. When it comes to pursuing an acting career (as opposed to planning to use a graduate degree for teaching), the reasons to go to graduate school for acting are: the training, the degree, the stage experience, the professional relationships, and the exposure to the industry that some of the programs provide to their graduates. With the exception of the degree, you can get these experiences in other ways, though it can be more difficult. Think about how you would achieve these things if you did not go to graduate school. You will audition differently if you have fully prepared for different outcomes than if you are just "seeing what happens."

Auditions for Stage Roles

Sometimes monologues are requested in the first rounds of auditions for specific roles in plays. The purpose is to gauge the actor's skill and also his work ethic—the degree of preparation evident in the audition may be what the auditors can expect on opening night. If the audition goes well, the actor may be asked to read scenes from the script. Or, he may be asked to come to a callback to read.

These auditions tend not to be held at the professional level in major cities. They frequently are held for school, college, and community theater plays, and often for summer stock, repertory and smaller regional theaters.

When auditioning actors for a specific role with monologues, auditors are looking for an actor who can play the role in *their* production of the play, and sometimes also for someone who is compatible (or contrasts) type-wise with actors who have already been cast.

Research the following questions: Who is producing the play? Who is the director? What is the producing history of the theater or producers?

You may also be able to benefit from finding out what the director's past credits have been. If, for example, the director specializes in updated versions of classics, and if the role being cast is classical, you might make sure to find a modern adaptation of a classical role from which to do a monologue. Is the director known for extremely physical productions? Contemporary comedy? All of these considerations can enter your decision-making process.

Assess the Role

What are the demands of the role being cast in:

- Physicality?

- Energy?

- Language skills?

- Movement and behavior?

- Period?

- Style?

- Personality?

- Sense of humor?

- Emotional range?

Find a monologue that addresses as many of these areas as possible, especially the ones your common sense tells you are most essential to playing the role.

Should You Do a Monologue from the Role?

Your monologue should show that you can play the role, but unless requested by your auditors, it should usually not be a monologue from the actual role being cast.

I say "usually" because nothing is absolute in casting, and because actors have won roles by doing a monologue from the part. But the often-heard advice *not* to do this exists, in my opinion, because when you audition with a monologue from the role, you are showing them a "finished product." The audition should show your *potential* to be involved in that director's rehearsal process and production of the play.

When you show a monologue from the role, you are more likely than not performing something other than what you would do after a rehearsal process with that director.

Nevertheless, it is possible that your performance will be close to the director's vision, or that the production has a very short rehearsal period and they will be glad to have an actor who is already halfway there. It's your call.

If you don't do a monologue from the role, you should examine the play being cast and any published audition requirements, and also address type, style, period, and length with your monologue choice.

It is wise to choose a monologue by the same playwright, or a playwright of a related style or period, that shows qualities close to the role being cast. For example, if a production of *Romeo and Juliet* is being cast, and they ask not to see monologues from the play, a young man wanting to be considered for Romeo should bring in another young romantic lead from a Shakespeare play to audition with. He should *not* bring in a darker, older Shakespearean lead like Iago or Richard III—this is an often-made mistake!

When a similar role by the same playwright does not exist, find a similar type of character by another playwright who wrote in a related period or style. The monologue role should be close to you in type; you should see yourself playing the part; it should be age-appropriate, and definitely from a play.

Auditions for Film Roles

It is not terribly frequent that actors are asked to perform monologues for film auditions, but it does happen, mostly for student films and short films. Many of the same guidelines apply as for auditioning for a specific theater role.

Find a monologue similar in spirit and style to the character you're auditioning for. It can be from a film, but it should not be too well known.

If your monologue is from a play, the language should match the style of the film being cast and should usually not sound theatrical at all.

Take note of the style and genre of the film being cast, and address the demands of the role being cast in physicality, energy, personality, sense of humor, and emotional range.

Make sure your audition is the size of a film reality, as opposed to a theatrical reality. The wide availability of consumer-level electronics means that almost everyone has access to some kind of video camera, so practice doing the monologue on-camera if you possibly can. Look just to the side of the lens—never directly into it. Experiment with a friend working the camera until it looks right and until you are used to performing the monologue this way.

General Auditions for a Professional Theater

In these general monologue auditions, theaters are looking to meet actors whom they might want to call in at a future time to read for roles in specific plays.

These auditions may happen on an individual basis, as a result of having met the casting director of the theater, or at a casting call organized by the theater.

General auditions are different from Equity Principal Auditions (which are described later), because these are auditions theaters choose to hold, as opposed to auditions the union requires of them.

Your goal should be to give an example of a kind of role you do well, within the range of genres and styles produced by that theater. You should resist any temptation to try to show *many* kinds of roles you feel you do well. Your monologue should be a piece you have received positive feedback on, not a stretch, and extremely close to you in playable age and range.

This is a perfect opportunity to study the theater's production history and find a monologue that interacts with the nature of some of the past work of that company. You might also find out if the theater's upcoming season has been announced, so that you can consider monologues by some of the playwrights they will be producing. However, you probably should not, for reasons discussed in "Auditions for Stage Roles," perform a monologue from a play the theater recently produced, or one they will be producing.

It is important to avoid overdone contemporary monologues, and the most famous 20th-century American roles, because they are seen so often at these kinds of auditions. Look for good, new writing, and lesser-known works by established writers.

Multi-Theater General Auditions

At these auditions, actors have the opportunity to audition for the summer and repertory seasons of many theaters at once. Both plays and musicals are cast from these auditions, but this discussion deals only with monologues, not with songs.

Auditors at multi-theater general auditions are often looking to cast repertory companies or whole seasons. They will want to see strong material that is solidly within the actor's casting range.

Audition times are generally very short—you often have only 90 seconds to show a song and monologue, or either one or two monologues. It's therefore extra-important for your monologues to be active and clear from the very first moment. Embrace the fact that these auditions are truly about getting a *taste*—not a whole meal—of what you can do. Callbacks are generally held on the same day. If called back, be prepared to show other, or longer, or more contrasting material in case you are asked to.

Since the audition will be for many theaters at once, you won't be able to tailor your material to a single aesthetic. You should instead keep in mind that the purpose of the audition is to show yourself playing the kinds of characters you would most likely be cast as. Therefore, considering type (leads vs. character parts) and featuring material that plays to your strengths are extremely important.

If not auditioning for musicals (and therefore with a song as one of your pieces), it is sometimes up to you to choose whether to do two 45-second monologues or one 90-second one. When wondering which option works most to your advantage, ask: Is your solidly-castable range large enough that doing two monologues is definitely required to show it? If you are most often cast in a certain way, meaning consistent types of leads, or consistent types of character parts, these auditions are probably not the place to try to break out of that. If, however, you know there is a part of your range that is strong but not obvious on first meeting, and that you want to be cast in more often, have monologues that show you can do those characters well. Practice your two short pieces until you are completely on top of them, and can consistently give each one its due.

Audiences for these theaters tend to support seasons of proven, mostly mainstream plays. A contemporary monologue choice could be a good role for you from a play that has been successfully produced in New York and is now making its way to the regional theaters. You can also do monologues from plays that have been regionally successful over the last several years.

If the contrast piece is classical, this is an opportunity to show that you know you would probably be cast as Ophelia as opposed to Kate, or Lady MacBeth as opposed to Viola (not to limit the classical choice to Shakespeare).

If the contrast monologue does not need to be classical, consider doing a good role for you from classic 20th-century drama, showing yourself handling period language and behavior.

If doing two monologues, definitely make one of them comedic. If doing one, do comedic or dramatic based on which you and others believe is more your strength.

It is important that some range be shown if you're doing two pieces for repertory theaters, so that auditors can see they can solve two problems with one actor. However, both pieces should be in your playable casting range, and the range should not be *so* large that auditors are left wondering, "Who is he?"

The websites of the holders of these auditions often have lists of overdone contemporary monologues that auditors do not wish to see again (and most are on my lists). Double-check these lists as you look for monologues.

Time your pieces so you know *for sure* that your audition fits into the time requirements. Time limits are strictly enforced, and actors are often cut off if their auditions run over.

Equity Principal Auditions (EPAs)

Actors' Equity Association is the stage actors' union in the United States. Equity theaters and the producers of Equity shows must hold Equity Principal Auditions, and they are open to Equity actors. Non-union actors may sometimes be seen at these auditions.

While I am in full support of EPAs in principle, I think it's important to note that this is an audition a theater or producing team *must* have, rather than one they choose to have.

The auditors are obligated to see all of the Equity actors who show up for the number of audition slots, as opposed to the auditions for which they call in actors they know of and specifically want to see.

Those watching the EPAs will be seeing dozens of actors per day, and often hundreds over the course of the auditions.

The reality in New York is that actors are not often cast in Broadway or Off-Broadway roles from these auditions. It can be rare that the actual director of the production is present at the EPAs.

All of this might sound like I think it's a waste of time to go to New York EPAs, but in many cases, I don't. The reasons to go include:

- There are theaters and directors who do cast from EPAs, including non-New York productions and tours holding their auditions here.

- To have your work seen. The artistic director's associate or casting director's assistant watching the auditions may herself be a director. If your monologue is a well-written, great piece for you that you enjoy doing, you will stand out.

- Theaters may save the pictures and résumés of the strongest performers and send them to the casting office for future reference (Atlantic does).

- For audition experience.

- To practice choosing material!

- If roles being cast are specialized in any way— including attributes such as height, weight, appearance, or ethnicity—or require certain talents or special skills you have, it is *always* worthwhile to go to the EPA.

Auditions for Newer Theater Companies

Included in this category are "fringe" and Off-Off Broadway types of companies, including those whose work might be called "experimental" or that embraces a particular comedic, artistic, social, or political credo. In addition to acting skill, these companies will be looking for actors who understand and share their artistic sensibilities and goals.

The audition is an opportunity for you and the company members to meet, and for you to show with your monologues how you feel you might harmonize with the company's work.

Because they may be looking for committed company members who will participate not only as actors, but also in the running or production work of the company, showing discipline and integrity in your approach to the audition will work very much in your favor.

For these auditions, you may have a wider than usual range of choices of audition material and interpretation: you may not have to pay the same attention to type that you do elsewhere, and you should definitely make sure that the material you choose excites you artistically. Base all such choices on your research of the company.

Before signing up to audition, you should make sure you have a very good sense of what the company is about, and that you can get behind the company's aesthetics and goals.

Theater Apprentice Program Auditions

Theaters need apprentices who can act, and who are motivated, reliable, hard working, in love with theater, team players, and enjoyable people to spend a summer, season, or year with.

As an actor, they want to know that you can hold your own in the apprentice productions, as well as possibly be tapped for small roles on the mainstage.

As an apprentice, they want to know that you are mature and easy to work with, and that they can totally rely on you to follow through on all of your responsibilities without having to be constantly checked on.

For your audition, you should attempt to give auditors a taste of both your personality and artistic sensibilities.

Your material should most probably be from plays.

You should consider a strong "Hello, this is me" monologue, and you should consider comedy you do well. Given that they're looking for people to work closely with during a pressured period of time, you should definitely avoid the more tortured and intense monologues.

You can also study the theater's production history, and consider material from the genres most often produced.

General Auditions for Film and Television Casting Directors

Casting directors hold general auditions to meet actors they don't know yet, and to meet unrepresented actors. Casting directors may also participate in meet-and-greets that actors pay for.

Your research is easy to start by going to www.imdb.com and entering the name of the casting director. Also search on Google.

Notice the *kinds* of things they've cast and see if there are any types of projects they've cast the most. Your material choice should probably be different for a casting director who has cast lots of edgy independent films than for one who mostly casts TV sitcoms.

A great question to ask as you do your research is, "In which projects have they cast someone like me?" Watching the roles in which they have cast actors similar to your type will give you ideas of the kinds of material that might be good to show them. This material should not be from the actual roles they've cast, because you run the risk of being compared to the original actor. Instead, let your choices be inspired by the *types* of roles you see that they've cast.

The reality in film and TV casting is that actors are often cast much closer to their face value than they are in theater.

Actors who are "allowed" by the mainstream industry to do roles beyond what might be perceived as their initial range have often had to fight for those opportunities, or they have first had to establish themselves as a particular kind of actor.

In any case, your first meeting with a film casting director is not the time to fight for your range. A "Hello, this is me" monologue you love is great for this kind of audition, because the most important thing to show the casting director on first meeting is *yourself.* This gives him a tangible base from which to start imagining you in various parts.

When doing a general audition for a casting director who primarily casts film and TV, it's all right to do a monologue from a film, but it should not be an iconic performance that everyone remembers. It's best to do a secondary character from a lesser-known film. You can also do good non-film monologues.

Monologues from plays can be fine, but the language should be straightforward and unstylized, and support you in showing ways you might be considered by that casting director. The monologue should work when done in a smaller size than you would in a theater audition.

This audition will most likely take place in an office, as opposed to a rehearsal room. Depending on the nature of the monologue, make the size and intimacy of your audition less theatrical and more appropriate for on-camera. Practice keeping your intensity and commitment while reducing the overall size of your performance. If possible, you should rehearse on-camera.

Meetings with Agents and Managers

The purpose of the agent or manager meeting is for them to see whether you are an actor they think they can work successfully with over a period of time.

The meeting is also of course for you to see if you think you can work with them. However, given the number of actors seeking representation, it is most usually the agents and managers who are doing the picking and choosing.

The process is subjective. Just because one agent or manager doesn't think she can work with a particular actor doesn't mean another one won't. The point is to find good chemistry, and mutual understanding and agreement on goals for your career.

Your research should include efforts to find out the size and reputation of the agency, and anything you can about the agent or manager's background. Not all of this information will be readily available. It also won't work in your favor to grill the agent or manager about any of these questions, or to take the attitude that "you're interviewing them." Finding out as much as you can will simply make you active, and will help orient you about who you will be talking to. It will also help you to gain information and perspective over the long term.

There are many books for actors written about how to meet, audition for, and work with agents (and sometimes managers).

Some are written by agents themselves. I actually suggest reading all of the books you can find. A terrific one to start with is by former agent and manager Brian O'Neil: *Acting as a Business*. Knowledge is power, and by reading you will get valuable perspectives on this important part of your professional life.

When it comes to showing monologues to agents and managers, I think you should do it when you are completely ready. It is a mistake to force yourself to find and learn new pieces because you have a meeting with an agent in a few days. You will have learned the monologues just for that meeting, and they are likely to be under rehearsed. Instead, pursue meeting with agents and managers when you have great pieces ready to show them.

How do you know when you're ready to do a monologue for an agent or manager?

- When you are fairly regularly being cast in roles you land without representation, and want to take your career to the next level.

- When you have researched what it means to have representation, and understand what agents and managers can and can't do for you.

- When you have spent time considering what kind of an actor you are and have clear professional goals you are ready to discuss.

- When you have monologues you are confident about, that show how you can be cast in professional theater productions, film projects, or television shows.

A good "Hello, this is me" monologue is ideal for a first meeting with an agent or manager, because it will help them get a clear sense of you. If you can do two pieces for them, consider doing a "Hello, this is me" that has some humor, and also a monologue close to your age and type that shows a little dramatic range. If comedy is your strength, that can be reflected in your second piece and your "Hello this is me" could be about a topic you are passionate about or find fascinating.

These are just suggestions. The goal is to have pieces that are strengths, close to you, and that bring you to life in specific, contrasting ways that the agent or manager can definitely see.

Remember that your goal is to spark their imagination about the *potential* of working with you—not to try to throw all of your goods out onto the table. Your pieces should be very well prepared. You should practice with rehearsal partners watching you, and practice performing your monologues in an office type of atmosphere.

You should also practice, with a rehearsal partner, saying hello and talking succinctly about your background and what you have been up to lately. It's also good to practice just chatting in a relaxed way about casual stuff—many actors say the best agent or manager conversations they've had have been about topics other than acting or the industry.

You should practice going from the chitchat into the pieces, and transitioning out of the monologues into more chatting, so that you are prepared for all of the possibilities that might come up. You should be prepared to talk about some of your personal background, training, and well-thought out professional goals.

Monologue Competitions

I have watched the Manhattan Monologue Slam[19] here in New York several times, and have formed the following opinions about choosing monologues for competitions. A competition monologue should:

- Be a good fit for the actor in age and type.

- Be great writing.

- Be either quite dramatic or very funny, not in between.

- Have a very clear journey from start to finish—not lots of side notes and meandering.

---

19 The Manhattan Monologue Slam is held monthly in New York at the time of this writing, and frequently in Los Angeles. It is a fantastic way to be seen by industry—when else do you get to audition in front of a happy, supportive audience of fellow actors who have had a drink? For more information, see Resources.

   While we're talking about the Slam, here are my two cents about how to choose a monologue for the 30-second slam that is the second half of the evening. Actors frequently think they have to find a 30-second monologue, or cut a longer monologue to 30 seconds. This often results in rushing to get the monologue out within the time limit and can hurt the actor's connection to the story. Instead, actors should do the first 30 seconds of a very good monologue. It's the old "leave them wanting more" trick. Do the first 30 seconds of a great monologue, at a reasonable pace, and your audience will beg for more.

- Not be written by the actor, unless he is a superb writer.

- Not be too gimmicky or full of props—this turns it into an "act" instead of truly a monologue.

- Most importantly, the monologue should be something you connect to, and therefore that will support you in acting truthfully in front of a live audience. The temptation at competitions is to push comedic or dramatic moments in an attempt to "be the best" and to win. This can lead an actor down the path of trying to get a reaction from the audience instead of telling a story. A monologue you're connected to will help you reveal the best of yourself as an actor.

At first look it might seem that the best competition pieces are comedic, because if done well there will be a definite vocal response from the audience. However, I have seen several dramatic performances win the Slam, because the bottom line is that an audience loves a well-told story, regardless of whether it's comedy or drama. An actor who truly commits to a good dramatic piece always gets a big response at the end.

Doing Monologues for Fun

Can you possibly imagine doing monologues for fun?

Director Carl Forsman spoke to the Atlantic Acting School students and asked, "When was the last time you read a play for fun?" Hardly anyone at the lecture, including faculty, could answer this question. (Carl regularly does read plays for fun. See his play list at www.monologueaudition.com.)

It's amazing how quickly and completely the things we originally did because they brought us joy, challenge, escape—*fun*—can become *work* that we therefore procrastinate about, once we've decided to pursue them seriously or professionally.

Another person I know who regularly does creative things for fun is Ze Frank. Ze is hard to describe. He is a comedian, speaker, writer, internet personality, web designer, musician, illustrator, teacher, and more. His website is www.zefrank.com, which has had well over 50 million hits in the last several years. The site features an astounding amount of his games, short films, collaborative projects, and writings.

We were lucky to have Ze appear in *The Monologue Audition Video (DVD)*. He hilariously plays the actor who does everything wrong at auditions. Shortly after we shot the DVD, Ze started his own daily internet show.[20] For one year, he made a new show every weekday, and put it on his site. Each morning

---

20 *The Show with Ze Frank*. Watch the episodes at www.zefrank.com.

he would write, shoot, and edit an episode and have it online by early afternoon.

Ze forced himself to do the show every day no matter how he felt, so occasionally you will see him performing with the flu. He even did shows when he was traveling on business. He attracted a huge worldwide audience, with whom he collaborated on many projects, such as playing chess and making an Earth Sandwich.[21] The show caught the attention of Hollywood, Ze signed with a top agency, and we now await his next big project. In the meantime, he continues to speak around the world on creativity and technology, and maintains a blog on which he often charges his audience to collaborate on new creative endeavors.

Carl Forsman loves plays so much that he started his own theater company, the highly respected Keen Company, so that he could direct and produce the plays of his favorite writers and eras.

I'm writing about Carl and Ze because they both do what I think artists must do in order to be happy and fulfilled: they actively create their own fun, instead of waiting for someone to let them. They have the creative habit. This has led to professional opportunities for each of them, such as Ze's movie deals and Carl's being made artistic director of the Dorset Theatre Festival.

My favorite episode of *The Show with Ze Frank* is called "Brain Crack."[22] According to Ze, Brain Crack is an unexecuted creative idea. His theory is that we get addicted to the *potential* of the idea—like it's crack—instead of actually executing the idea and seeing if it is any good.

---

21 Two slices of bread were simultaneously placed on exactly opposite points on the globe (in Spain and in New Zealand), turning the earth, for that moment, into a sandwich. The Earth Sandwich is documented at www.zefrank.com/sandwich.

22 See www.monologueaudition.com/braincrack to watch "Brain Crack" and to read about Brain Crack that actors have executed since being inspired by that episode.

What are *your* Brain Cracks when it comes to acting, auditioning, and monologues? What do you imagine doing, but haven't taken action on yet?

Could monologues be a way that you regularly have artistic fun?

Expanding Your Range

This chapter contains guidelines for choosing monologues to improve your acting skills and increase your casting range. You can use monologues to expand your range by:

- Choosing pieces that require you to access parts of yourself that you find difficult to express;

- Experimenting with roles that feature sides of your personality that others don't often see;

- Meeting certain performing fears head on by choosing monologues that challenge you in specific, personal ways;

- Working on character types that are new to you;

- Studying specific styles of acting you would love to master, and choosing pieces in those styles;

- Finding monologues to feature your work on new accents and dialects.

Increasing Emotional Accessibility

Sometimes there are parts of the self that are difficult for an actor to access in his acting. To examine this for yourself, you can ask:

- What parts of myself am I comfortable revealing? Which characters have I done—in monologues, scenes, or plays—that have expressed these parts of myself?

- What parts of myself am I *least* comfortable revealing?

Here are some possible areas to address:

Power	Fear	Sincerity
Assertiveness	Terror	Serenity
Aggression	Nervousness	Surrender
Cruelty		
	Sadness	Giddiness
Righteousness	Grief	Mischievousness
Pride	Weakness	Recklessness
Self-satisfaction		
	Strength	Humor
Joy	Maturity	Deadpan/dryness
Wonder	Wisdom	Sarcasm
Delight	Authority	Silliness
Love		Bawdiness
Tenderness	Flirtation	Clowning
Vulnerability	Seductiveness	
Bashfulness	Sensuality	
Awe		

Once you have identified a quality to work on, you can begin your search for monologues and characters that require you to express it. Involve rehearsal partners in this effort. Ideally, each of you will be working on expanding your emotional accessibility, and supporting each other in doing so.

Following are two exercises I give as assignments in my advanced monologue class. They can be part of tackling the previous suggestions about expanding emotional range, or they can be considered on their own. Their purpose is to challenge actors' perceptions of what they can do—not in general, but by connecting the challenge to a specific characteristic, fear, or belief from within the actor's own personality.

The Secret Identity Monologue

I love this exercise. Choose a monologue that reflects a part of yourself that you do not often—if ever—show anyone. The monologue can express a fantasy of who you would love to be, or a fear you have about how you might appear to others. It could also express a certain point of view or sense of humor that you only share with one or two people. It could also be a side of yourself you're not proud of. I won't cite examples of the kinds of monologues actors have brought into class as their Secret Identities, because it's important that the monologue choice come deeply from *you*. Only you know what your secret identities are. I will say that actors who do this assignment frequently believe they would never actually audition with the monologues they choose as their secret identities, but very often, they can.

The Challenge Monologue

In his wonderful book *The War of Art: Break Through the Blocks and Win Your Inner Creative Battles* (see Resources), Steven Pressfield talks about how actors are drawn to the roles that most terrify them. This exercise is about choosing a monologue that is a direct personal challenge. It's also about being willing to pick something you might fail at. You will know you've chosen the right monologue when you feel nervous-to-terrified at the prospect of working on it. Like the secret identity monologue, the challenge monologue is also a completely personal choice.

What may be a challenge for one actor may not be for another. Some examples from my class: An actor who absolutely hated her singing voice did a monologue that started with a song. A man who had been told by a director that he was horrible at Shakespeare—and who had subsequently avoided doing or even seeing Shakespeare for ten years—did a monologue from *Hamlet* (and performed it beautifully). You should be drawn to the Challenge monologue but also be afraid you can't quite pull it off.

These are all extremely powerful exercises and I invite you to try them. It is artistically thrilling to deliberately work out of your comfort zone. Often, an actor's most exciting work will happen when she feels the least safe.

If you choose pieces that are true challenges for you, and work as hard as you can to meet them, you will be a different actor than you were before, regardless of the final result.

These monologues will not always be ones you can audition with, but surprisingly often, they can be. Once you have successfully met a challenge, you own it. Your confidence and fearlessness will increase, and you will want to challenge yourself more.

Character Types

I once directed a play in which the female lead was an ambitious, sexy, working class young woman who got the opportunity to become a corporate executive. Most of the women who auditioned accentuated the sexual and blue-collar nature of the character in the first auditions. For the callbacks, we asked the agents to tell the actors to wear business suits and adjust their behavior to show they could also behave convincingly in the corporate environment the young woman finds herself in later in the play.

I think it's a very useful exercise to identify which types of characters come most easily to you (both in look and manner); which you can pull off with believable changes in your speech, movement, and behavior; and, which types are probably out of your playing range. The below types and professions allow for many different kinds of personalities and styles of playing. It can be a fun exercise to consider what you would have to do to portray your own versions of some of these characters convincingly. You can find monologues that express the kinds of characters you would most enjoy playing, *and* the ones you are likely to be cast as.

CEO	Killer
Suburban mom, dad, or teen	Holy man or woman
Street person	King or Queen
Schoolteacher	Bohemian
Deli worker	Politician
Rock star	Cutthroat lawyer
Science or computer nerd	Sorority girl or frat guy
Soldier	Factory worker
Secretary	Gangster
Beach bum	Society man or woman
Doctor	Police officer
Party girl or boy	Farmer
Gambler	Professor
Professional athlete	Poet

Acting Styles and Period Movement

There are many theater and film styles other than contemporary naturalism. These can include drawing room comedies, farce, Commedia dell'arte, Theatre of the Absurd, Restoration comedies, film noir, screwball comedies, and movies and plays set in historical periods. Each period and style has its own rules of movement, speech, and behavior that need to be studied carefully in order to fully realize the characters. Also within these styles are characters of varying classes, types and personalities.

You can make studies of characters in the styles, genres, and periods that most appeal to you. This is as easy as watching particular plays, renting films, and viewing tapes or DVDs of past theater productions. You can also research styles and periods in books and online. Find monologues that you can use as vehicles for working on the characters.

If you want to develop professional-level abilities to move, speak, and act in roles of different styles and time periods, I highly recommend training in dedicated programs, such as Actors Movement Studio in New York, with teachers who are experts at teaching actors period movement and behavior. (See Resources.)

Accents and Regionalisms

You never know you can truly do an accent until you can keep the accent while committing fully to your acting. Therefore, monologues are perfect vehicles for practicing acting in an accent, regionalism, or language other than your own. You can study accents with teachers, in taped courses, and online. (See Resources.)

Prioritize the monologues you work on for accents by considering your casting range. Pay attention to other factors discussed earlier about age, type, subject matter, and appropriateness for particular auditions. Identify people who can give you feedback about how well you are doing the accent.

Solving Performance Problems

Monologues clearly reveal an actor's performing habits and problems, because there is no scene partner to distract attention or take up the slack. *All* of us have physical and vocal habits, and the good news is that you can use monologue work to identify yours, and to help you eliminate the ones that lessen the power of your performances.

Below are descriptions of the kinds of vocal and physical habits I see most often, and some suggested ways of addressing them. Please note, however: if you are serious about acting, I highly recommend that all of the vocal and physical suggestions in this chapter be worked on in conjunction with the best training available to you in these areas.

Voice Issues

Vocally, your goals should be to have consistent vocal support, appropriate volume, and full range of expression. Some people have naturally resonant and expressive voices, but all actors who are dedicated to their craft should study so that they can use, support, and maintain their voices to maximum levels throughout their careers.

I believe you must study with a qualified teacher, both to develop the power and beauty of your voice, and to avoid damaging your voice through incorrect use over time. Once you understand your own particular vocal issues, including breathing, physical alignment, tensions, and placement, you can choose monologues that will help you work on these areas.

If you are acting at a pre-professional level, you may have not studied speaking voice yet. If this is the case, you should concentrate on being heard and voicing sounds fully when you act and when you work on monologues. If you are acting and auditioning on a professional or aspiring-to-be-professional level however, consistent voice work should be a part of your daily life and preparation. In her interview for *The Monologue Audition Video (DVD)*, director Amanda Charlton said:

> *"I really notice the people who have [vocal] training and the people who don't. The people who don't can't control their breath. Sometimes when someone is especially nervous, the voice rises a couple of octaves and gets thin, and then you'll talk to them afterwards and they have this great rich voice. So that's a great indicator of someone who doesn't have training. And that's an easy, fixable thing and a lot of people don't take the time to do it. It makes a big difference."*

Voice work is not just for theater actors either—professional actors get vocal coaching for film roles all the time. Voice is the primary building block of your craft.

To support your vocal progress with monologues, start with a simple contemporary piece, and get feedback from a partner or teacher on whether you are consistently vocally supported, and therefore heard and understood throughout the monologue. You can then build to more complex material and language that will require increased breath support to sustain longer thoughts and more intricate expressions in the writing.

I'm not suggesting specific monologues to work on here, because the choices should come from your own preferences and self-assessments. Read different monologues you like out loud, and notice how difficult or easy you find them on a vocal level.

Start with the simpler pieces, and build to the more difficult ones as your vocal power and expression increase.

Speech Issues

For speech, the first question is: Can we effortlessly understand every word you are saying? Speech issues I hear often include:

- Mumbling. One example: running words together, such as saying "Ummunna" instead of "I'm going to."

- Regionalisms and speech patterns that contribute to not saying words clearly. For example, pronouncing "ing" endings as "een," so we hear "runneen, walkeen, and swimmeen." I also often hear actors add "sh" to words that begin with "str," so we hear "shtraight," "shtreet," or "shtrawberry." These are only a couple of examples.

- Simply not having speech skills at enough of a level to completely take advantage of the power of the language the writer has given you. All plays were written to be spoken out loud—they are poetry. The sounds of the individual words can be as important as their meanings. Having clear speech means you are truly committing to what you are saying. Neglecting speech and articulation cuts the power of what you are saying in half.

To practice speech, you can select a series of monologues that start with simple articulation challenges, and then build to more and more difficult ones. The difficult monologues don't always have to be classical—you'll find that some contemporary playwrights like Nicky Silver make great demands on an actor's speech in monologues. It is incredibly beneficial to practice monologues for speech on your own, out loud, drilling them for clear sounds and articulation. Go slowly enough that you are never speaking more quickly than you can clearly articulate. As you gain more and more command of the language, you can vary your speed depending on the rhythm of the text and your interpretation.

The point is not to become "speechy," but to be clear and in command of what you are saying. Then, practice acting the monologue full-out with a partner watching, so that you can tell how much of your practice is sticking. Ask your partner to gently raise his hand whenever he has trouble understanding you, or whenever he hears you doing a specific sound you have chosen to address. Stop, fix the sound, and go on. Practice until you are always clearly understood throughout your performance.

The desire to act *is* the desire to be understood. Early in his life as an actor, William H. Macy changed his diction all by himself by making a personal decision to eliminate his regionalism and to always speak clearly. You can hear his voice all the time in television voiceovers. Sidney Poitier developed his diction by listening to radio announcers. And the great Irish stage actress Anna Manahan gave our students wonderful advice when she told them, "I always finish every word I say."

You can also choose monologues to support yourself in practicing—or overcoming—accents and regionalisms. If possible, have someone who is a native speaker of the accent you wish to speak in read your monologue into a tape recorder, without acting it. When you practice, note the rhythm and emphasis as well as the sounds. There are also some very helpful free accent websites you can visit. (See Resources.)

Language Execution Problems

Sometimes an actor will have good voice production and diction, but will still have language execution problems that make his speaking hard to follow. The most common of these problems are:

- Breaking up language—inserting stops and breaths in the middle of thoughts.

- Not knowing which words in a verse line or sentence are most important to emphasize for meaning to be clear (and therefore which words *not* to emphasize—or to "throw away").

I hear both of these issues when students do Shakespeare, but also when they perform monologues by modern writers. To address them, choose a monologue with fairly complex language. Speak the monologue out loud, without acting it. Practice sustaining energy all the way through a thought or line. Find out where you need to take breaths, and set them. Experiment, and then make conscious choices about which words you should emphasize to make the thoughts clear.

It is extremely helpful to do this with one or more partners, focusing on the same text, and to slowly, line by line, practice articulating each full thought, while also experimenting with emphasis. Listening to other actors make this exploration will strengthen your own abilities. Once your language execution is easy to understand on a non-acted level, practice performing the monologue in front of others and get their feedback about any decrease in clarity that happens when you act it.

Flatness and Downward Inflection

Many American regionalisms sound quite flat compared to other English-speaking accents such as English, Irish, Scottish, or Australian, to name a few. Along with this, many Americans tend to downwardly-inflect when they speak—meaning that overall, the tone drops down in pitch as the speaker progresses through a line or a thought. This tendency can kill the momentum of a monologue and make the piece sound like it "never gets off the ground." To address this issue, you can consciously work a monologue for inflection and tone. Progressing line by line, reading without fully acting the piece, identify which words are important to lift tonally in order to drive the momentum forward. This work can go hand in hand with your work on language execution.

Physical Fidgets

I call all unproductive physical performing habits "fidgets," and believe (except when a medical condition is present) that they are manifestations of an actor not fully discharging his impulses when he acts.

Fidgets weaken your performance because they distract from the language and the truth of the moment. I tell students to work on fidgets in the following ways:

- Consider fidgets a good sign—their presence means you have energy, and that you are affected by the story you are telling. It's just that you want to be in more control of how you express your impulses.

- Always give yourself a positive direction to substitute for the fidget. Instead of cursing yourself for thrusting your head forward again, substitute the positive instruction to "use my height."

- It's impossible to act while trying to monitor your own fidgets. Instead, always work with a partner who will be your outside eye. You will solve your fidgeting problems much more quickly, and you can trade the favor with your partner.

Here is a list of the physical fidgets I see most often, accompanied by a positive instruction you can give yourself once your partner has pointed a fidget out. As you can see, the positive instructions add up to qualities that make for powerful, focused acting:

- **Shifting weight side to side when acting.** "Use your stillness."

- **Parking the weight habitually on one hip (unless this is a clear choice for one specific place in a monologue).** "Stand on both your feet."

- **Creeping with unplanned, half-committed steps while speaking—rather than making a clear, definite move.** "Make each movement count: either move fully, or use your stillness."

- **"Conducting" or beating out language rhythms with the head and/or arms.** "Let your *voice* do the rhythm."

- **Flopping hands down to the sides.** "Finish every impulse completely."

- **Half-hearted gestures.** "Use either a full gesture, or complete stillness."

- **Rubbing fingers or hands together.** "Use the power of stillness in your hands."

- **Jutting the head, neck, or upper body forward.** "Use your height."

- **Raising the chin too high.** "Drop your chin and invite us in."

- **Nodding the head "yes," or shaking the head**

"no" frequently while speaking. "Find stillness and power with your head."

- **Looking down at the floor a lot.** "Let the audience see into your eyes."

- **Blinking excessively.** "Keep your attention out and connected to the person you are speaking to."

As you can see, there are many little ways an actor can dispel tension or wriggle out of facing a difficult moment in the monologue. Your acting power will increase exponentially if you work patiently to re-route the energy of your fidgets into either total, engaged stillness, or deliberate and purposeful movement.

Fidgets tend to come out the most when your mind is on acting the monologue, so I suggest using the following process to work on them:

- Identify a fidget you want to work on, and tell your partner what it is.

- Only work on one fidget at a time.

- Before you start the monologue, practice deliberately doing the fidget, and then making the correction a few times.

- Ask your partner to raise her hand as soon as she sees you doing the fidget, and to keep it there until you stop doing it.

- When you see the hand, *stay in the story,* and make the appropriate positive adjustment while continuing to act the monologue fully. *Don't* create the habit of stopping and starting. Your acting will become much more powerful if you *include* the moment of correcting the fidget.

- When you have made the adjustment, your partner lowers her hand.

Again, if you want to bring your physical use to a professional level, there is no substitute for training with good teachers that will make your movements more efficient, graceful, and powerful. This can include study of Alexander technique, dance, and various actor movement training systems.

However, I have seen actors go a long way towards overcoming their unhelpful physical habits by working patiently with rehearsal partners.

Vocal Fidgets

All vocal fidgets prevent the impulse from coming out fully *on* the line, *with* the language, and weaken your acting. I find actors do them to hide uncertainty and vulnerability—your greatest potential moments as an actor.

If you find you do any of these vocal fidgets, work with a partner who will bring your attention to it by raising his hand as you are acting.

- "Huffing"—exhaling or sighing before speaking. I call this "starting with a flat tire." The "huff" is always the real impulse. Express that impulse *with the line*.

- "Tsking" as the mouth is opened, before actually speaking the line.

- Adding half-voiced sounds and words to the text, such as "Yeah," "Um," "Uhh," and "I mean." This is a terrible habit that drives playwrights bananas. Do the impulse *on* the actual line, and don't add extra words or sounds.

Videotaping For the Not-Faint-of-Heart

Realizing how much unproductive physical and vocal habits hurt his performance can quickly result in an actor's becoming dedicated to fixing them.

I once had a student who, like many new actors, was shoving his head forward a lot while acting. I had him step out to watch, and had another student come up and say one of the first student's lines while deliberately jutting his head forward. I then had the second student say the line with physical straightness. Once the first student saw this huge difference, and realized how weak the habit made him appear on stage, he immediately corrected himself and was very consistently straight and powerful in the rest of the work he did in class.

Videotaping, if you can possibly stand to watch yourself, can help you get this invaluable outside perspective on what your fidgets really look like. If you do have someone videotape you, I suggest the following process:

- Have your partner videotape you from the side first, while you act the monologue. Tell them to get a full body shot, head to toe, so that you can see what you are doing with your alignment when you are fully committing to your acting.

- When playing back, do it silently, so that you are not distracted by the sound of your own voice. Focus on your alignment, your head and neck position, and how you are engaging your whole body when you act.

- Videotape from the front and playback silently, so that you can see if you are drawing your focus and chin up too high. Notice whether you are committing to clear gestures instead of half-hearted ones, or flopping hands down at your sides repeatedly.

- If your partner says you're doing vocal fidgets, listen back just to the sound, so you can clearly hear when you might be huffing, or adding extra words or sounds.

- Use the video camera as a positive tool, in a spirit of self-support. Film at regular intervals so you can see your progress as you work on particular issues.

Have 20 Monologues

I hope by now I've convinced you to make searching for and working on monologues a regular part of your artistic and business life.

Procrastination is the enemy of all monologue finding and preparation. It will be hard to build a repertoire without consistent practice, and productive rehearsals, both on your own and with others. Again, I highly recommend Flylady's[23] system for creating effective routines.

Let's say you do have some good routines in place. How should you go about building your repertoire of twenty monologues?

Why 20 Monologues?

Well, mostly because twenty is such a nice, round, impressive number. Imagine how it would feel to know that you could do twenty monologues. And not just *any* twenty monologues, but twenty that are great pieces for you, and that showcase your strengths in a variety of auditions.

Twenty means you are really serious. An actor who is lucky enough not to hate monologues and their preparation might, over the course of a few years, build up a collection of eight or ten pieces. But I think we would all agree that the actor who can do twenty has decided to truly put his money where his mouth

---

23 See "Why Flylady Is Great for Actors" at www.monologueaudition.com.

is. We know he is committed; we know he is extremely disciplined; we know he loves his craft, and we know he is willing to go the extra mile—qualities that are very much needed in a business this competitive.

Choosing Your 20

I think each repertoire should be as unique as the actor who performs it, and that it should evolve as a result of regular reading, researching, thinking, and rehearsing over a period of time. Don't rush. Take your time and enjoy the process. Here are questions to ask yourself as you consider *your* twenty monologues:

- What kinds of auditions do you currently go on?

- Do you have monologues you are happy with for those auditions?

- What other kinds of monologues would you ideally have for those auditions?

- What kinds of monologue auditions do you expect to be going on in the future?

- What kinds of pieces would you ideally have for *those* auditions?

- What monologue auditions would you love to go on?

- What kinds of pieces would you ideally have for *those* auditions?

- Who are your most favorite playwrights?

- What are your favorite styles of movies?

- What are your favorite styles of theater?

- What are current strengths that you have?

- What monologues would help you show those strengths?

- What special skills do you have?

- What monologues could help you showcase those skills?

- What new skills would you like to work on?

- Do you have a few great "Hello, this is me" monologues?

- Do you have a few strong dramatic pieces?

- Do you have monologues that show the kinds of comedy you perform best?

- Which classic characters are *yours*?

- Do you have monologues that truly express things that you want to say about the world?

- Do you have monologues that are very close to you?

- Do you have monologues that show unexpected ways you could be cast?

- Do you have a collection of monologues that are good representations of your casting range?

- Do you have monologues that feature your ethnicity or background?

- What are your acting goals?

- Do you have monologues that reflect those goals?

- Do you have monologues from your dream roles?

As you can see, answering and considering these questions can easily turn into some concrete goal setting.

I can't emphasize enough that the best way to build up a killer repertoire is to take small, manageable steps, and to slowly build regular rehearsal routines and practices.

Here is a helpful repertoire-building tool. In my class, actors break down their monologues into sections, and record their analytical and physical choices for each section on a chart. The charts become invaluable records of their interpretations of each monologue they work on. If they don't audition with a particular monologue for a while, they can always go back to the chart to remember their choices, which makes brushing up on the monologue a quick and simple task.

The 20 Monologue Challenge

Years ago, to see if someone would really do it, I told my NYU classes that if anyone could do twenty monologues in a row, I would buy them dinner. Some time passed, and the next year one of that group, Karen Benelli, did do twenty monologues for me.

She gave me a list, and proceeded to perform all of the monologues in a row, with simple transitions between them. She did an excellent, unhesitating job and I was extremely impressed. I congratulated her, and I did buy her dinner. Karen is in *The*

Monologue Audition Video (DVD), and speaks of her experience doing the twenty monologues. She also wrote me a letter about how the challenge affected her auditioning life, which is excerpted below.

I adapted the offer so that it would be more useful to current students and alumni. Anyone who has ever studied monologues with me is eligible. If they do twenty monologues, I will no longer buy dinner, but I will take notes on each monologue, and go over the notes with them in detail after the performance—a free coaching session (and I don't usually coach privately).

As of this writing, only two other actors, Kate Kirby and Katherine Alt Keener, have done the challenge. It was a thrill and a pleasure to see them both. Their long-term payoffs from doing the challenge were probably much like Karen Benelli's. In Karen's letter, written a year after she did the challenge, she said the benefits were:

- *"First, the obvious—I have twenty prepared monologues under my belt. While I admit that right now I no longer remember them well enough to do in seamless succession, I still have them in a folder—-typed, blocked, and analyzed—and I could easily whip one into shape in an evening.*

- *Doing the exercise helps you realize which monologues are your strongest. About five stood out as being effortless and comfortable; another five felt awkward and pushed; the other ten fell somewhere in the middle.*

- *Breaking down, blocking, and analyzing a monologue gets a great deal easier after so much practice.*

- *Finding 20 different pieces forces you to be resourceful and look for monologues in unexpected places—slam poetry, Anne Frank's diary, one-man shows—no excuses for wimping out and buying a monologue book!*

- *Doing a large span of material at once allows you to notice any unintentional physical habits (e.g., was it a discomfort with that gesture or monologue that made me speed up and lock my knees, or am I doing it across the board?).*

- *And, after doing 20 monologues in a row, walking into an audition and doing one or two is unfathomably easy!"*

Afterword

Thank you for the opportunity to share these thoughts with you. This book has been a Brain Crack project for me for several years. I get asked so often which monologue an actor should do for a particular audition. The question comes from actors, students, and online from visitors to my website. This book is a collection of answers to that question. If you are an actor, I sincerely hope it helps you not only to find effective monologues for auditions, but also to make your long-term monologue work enjoyable, empowering, and fruitful. Please use my website as a resource, and feel free to contact me with questions and feedback.

Websites

KAREN'S WEBSITE

www.monologueaudition.com

Includes articles, actor resources, the Overdone Monologue Survey, audition advice, my books and DVD, links, and more.

PLAY SOURCES

www.newdramatists.org

The site of the invaluable New Dramatists organization in New York, a wonderful place to search for contemporary monologues.

www.playscripts.com

Playscripts publishes new plays and provides access to the scripts for browsing via their website – an ideal way to read plays before you buy, if you have little access to plays in your area.

www.dramabookshop.com

The website of New York's only dedicated theater and show business bookstore. Browse and buy plays and acting books, read the blog, and join the mailing list to hear about events and new releases.

www.dramatists.com

The website of play publisher Dramatists Play Service. Browse and buy plays on the site. You can also search by state for productions of DPS-published plays around the USA.

www.samuelfrench.com

In addition to thousands of plays, Samuel French also publishes books on acting technique, monologue collections and more.

MONOLOGUE SOURCES

www.themoth.org

The Moth is a not-for-profit storytelling organization. You can read all about the Moth on the site, and order CDs of great Moth stories.

www.whysanity.net/monos

Colin's huge movie monologue page. A great resource.

www.theonion.com

Look for first-person articles and mock interviews to use as monologue sources. You can find very funny pieces that are worth the search.

www.craigslist.org/about/best/all

The Best of Craig's List, voted by readers. Not everything you find will make a good monologue, but there are gems.

www.storycorps.net

This extraordinary not-for-profit project has recorded the personal stories of tens of thousands of people. There are extraordinary stories from ordinary people that can make beautiful monologues. On the site, you can listen to stories, and find the book *Listening Is an Act of Love*, a collection of first-person stories from the project.

RESEARCH TOOLS

www.doollee.com
This incredibly comprehensive site lists thousands of playwrights and their plays, and links for purchasing the plays.

www.findaplay.com
This search service created by Playscripts, Inc. will tell you the publisher of any published play.

www.imdb.com
The Internet Movie Database. Search for casting directors, and roles actors have played.

www.ibdb.com
The Internet Broadway Database. Research Broadway plays, playwrights, actors, directors, and casting directors.

www.lortel.org/LLA_archive
The Internet Off-Broadway Database. Research Off-Broadway plays, playwrights, actors, directors, and casting directors.

SHOWBIZ SAVVY

www.timeout.com/newyork/section/theater
The website of the weekly magazine *Time Out New York*, which always has the most complete theater listings for New York City. Read articles on theater productions and artists, and know what

is playing in New York. There are also *Time Out* magazines for hundreds of other American and international cities.

www.tcg.org/publications
The site for *American Theatre* magazine, a great way to stay current with what is happening in American theaters across the country. Excellent articles, publications and other resources.

www.playbill.com
Playbill magazine online. Another resource for staying current with theater in New York, the United States, and internationally.

www.backstage.com
Website of *Backstage East* and *Backstage West* magazines. The industry standard for actor information of all kinds.

TRAINING AND COACHING

www.atlanticactingschool.org
Our school has full time conservatory programs, a New York University undergraduate training studio, part time acting classes, voice and movement programs, spring and summer intensives in New York City, child and teen drama classes, and also holds acting classes in Los Angeles.

www.actorsmovementstudio.com
The place in New York City to study period movement by making full use of the actor's physical instrument. Run by master teacher Janice Orlandi, a longtime protégé of the legendary Loyd Williamson, AMS features Williamson technique, Michael Chekov's teachings, Fitzmaurice voice work and more.

www.actingsuccessnow.com
I highly recommend Robert and Michelle Colt's New York and Los Angeles seminars for actors. Learn powerful tools that enhance your ability to use your own acting and audition techniques the most positively and fully.

www.capesco.com
Capes Coaching is a wonderful New York career coaching center for actors and artists. They offer practical classes and one-on-one coaching with industry professionals based on your needs: from pursuing representation to graduate school audition preparation.

www.charlestuthill.com
Charles is the best acting and audition coach I know, and his website has lots of useful information.

www.getthinforthecamera.com
Holistic health counselor Donna Sonkin is dedicated to making actors happy, healthy, and glowing in their roles and auditions. Her site is packed with helpful information for all, and New York area actors (and others) can take her classes and work with her one-on-one.

www.thenetworknyc.com
The Network introduces New York area actors to agents, managers and casting directors, and provides industry knowledge through coaching and classes. They stand out with their small class sizes, lower fees, and the personalized attention of their free ongoing one-on-one consultations.

http://web.mac.com/maryannadennard
Website of Mary Anna Austin Dennard, whose students have been accepted to every major undergraduate training program in the country. She coaches both in person and long distance via iChat and Skype.

ACCENT RESOURCES

These two sites feature samples of people speaking English in just about any accent you can think of from around the world:

http://accent.gmu.edu
The Speech and Accent Archive.

http://web.ku.edu/idea
The International Dialects of English Archive.

MANHATTAN MONOLOGUE SLAM

www.mmslam.com
Site of the Galinsky brothers' Manhattan Monologue Slam, held monthly in New York and regularly in Los Angeles.

INSPIRATION AND FUN

www.zefrank.com
Check out Ze's amazing collection of short films, games, art, musings, and collaborative projects, as well as all of the episodes of The Show with Ze Frank.

Books

Acting As a Business: Strategies for Success
By Brian O'Neil
An invaluable, highly practical book on all aspects of being a professional actor, written by a former agent and manager, and current teacher and coach.

How to Be a Working Actor
By Mari Lyn Henry and Lynne Rogers
An excellent "Bible of the Biz." A great starting place for reading about entering the profession written by two very experienced ladies who love actors.

The Monologue Audition: A Practical Guide for Actors
By Karen Kohlhaas, Foreword by David Mamet
My step-by-step approach to directing, acting and auditioning with monologues.

The Organized Actor
By Leslie Becker
For regularly auditioning actors, Leslie's incredibly useful organizer includes marketing tips, an audition log, calendar, goal setting, inspiration and more. Available on her website, www.organizedactor.com.

The War of Art: Break Through Your Blocks
and Win Your Inner Creative Battles
By Steven Pressfield
A beautiful, useful, insightful book about living and working
as an artist.

The Monologue Audition Video (DVD)

Nine New York actors, comedian Ze Frank, and I show you how to Direct, Act, and Audition with monologues. We take you through each step of my monologue rehearsal technique, and show how to confidently handle your audition room entrances, exits, and interactions.

Seven industry professionals who have seen thousands and thousands of monologue auditions comment throughout the DVD:

- Arthur Bartow, New York University Undergraduate Drama artistic director

- Amanda Charlton, Williamstown Theatre Festival associate director

- Carl Forsman, Keen Company and Dorset Theatre Festival artistic director

- Mari Lyn Henry, talent manager and author of *How to Be a Working Actor*

- Christian Parker, Atlantic Theater Company associate artistic director

- Todd Thaler, casting director

- Charles Tuthill, actor, teacher and coach

The 120 minute full-color DVD includes a documentary-style feature, 30 minutes of bonus industry interviews, and downloadable study aids.

In the DVD:

- Industry professionals discuss what they like— and don't like—to see in auditions.

- Actors and industry professionals share problems and successes with material choice.

- We show you how to stage a monologue effectively so that your story is told well and your body knows what to *do* when you go in the audition room.

- We show you how to act spontaneously and truthfully off of "no one," because most auditors do not want you to act monologues to them.

- We show you how to make positive and confident entrances and exits.

- Actors demonstrate appropriate and comfortable ways to chat and interact with auditors before and after their monologue.

- We show you how to transition between two monologues.

- Ze Frank hilariously demonstrates common auditioning mistakes.

- We show you mock auditions that throw challenges at the actors, and demonstrate how to meet those challenges with confidence and ease.

- I take the actors through a powerful way to evaluate and benefit from each audition you do.

- The industry professionals provide additional commentary on clothing choices, audition room behavior, acting school and graduate school auditions, material choices and the most outrageous auditions they've ever seen!

Featuring Karen Benelli, David Beukema, Daniel Deferarri, Hadley Fitzgerald, Andre Harris, Jason Markouc, Adepero Oduye, Tamara Lovatt-Smith, and Riji Suh. Written and directed by Karen Kohlhaas. Produced by Karen Kohlhaas and Derrick Widmark.

Watch trailers and order the DVD at

www.monologueaudition.com

About the Author

Karen Kohlhaas is a theater director, teacher, and author who has been teaching her unique approach to monologues and auditioning since 1993. She is a founding member of New York's Atlantic Theater Company and a senior teacher at the Atlantic Acting School. Karen has directed for Atlantic, and also for the New York Shakespeare Festival/Public Theater, The Alley Theatre, Ars Nova, The Montreal Comedy Festival, St. Luke's Theatre, Naked Angels, Ensemble Studio Theatre, New Dramatists, the Practical Theatre Company in Sydney, Australia and others. Her short films have been seen at festivals in the United States and abroad. Karen is the author of *The Monologue Audition: A Practical Guide for Actors* (foreword by David Mamet), *The Monologue Audition Teacher's Manual*, and is the director, writer and co-producer of the DVD *The Monologue Audition Video*. She also writes articles for *Backstage* magazine. Her website for actors is www.monologueaudition.com. In addition to her classes at the Atlantic Acting School, Karen teaches private monologue workshops, classes in directing, and "Fearless Cold Reading & Audition Technique."